TO PAY
OR NOT
TO PAY

INSIDER SECRETS TO

BEATING CREDIT CARD

DEBT AND CREDITORS

Stanley G. Hilton, J.D., M.B.A.

ADAMS MEDIA
AVON, MASSACHUSETTS

Published by
Adams Media, an F+W Publications Company
57 Littlefield Street, Avon MA 02322 U.S.A.
www.adamsmedia.com

ISBN: 1-58062-944-X

Printed in the United States of America.

J   I   H   G   F   E   D   C   B   A

Library of Congress Cataloging-in-Publication Data
Hilton, Stanley G.
To pay or not to pay / Stanley G. Hilton.
p.   cm.
ISBN 1-58062-944-X
1. Debtor and creditor—United States—Popular works.
2. Debt relief—United States—Popular works. I. Title.

KF1501.Z9H55 2003
346.7307'7—dc21
2003004472

This publication is designed to provide accurate and authoritative information with regard to the subject matter covered. It is sold with the
understanding that the publisher is not engaged in rendering legal,
accounting, or other professional advice. If legal advice or other expert
assistance is required, the services of a competent professional person
should be sought.
—From a *Declaration of Principles* jointly adopted
by a Committee of the American Bar Association
and a Committee of Publishers and Associations

Many of the designations used by manufacturers and sellers to distin-
guish their products are claimed as trademarks. Where those designations appear in this book and Adams Media was aware of a trademark
claim, the designations have been printed with initial capital letters.

This book is available at quantity discounts for bulk purchases.
For information, call 1-800-872-5627.

CONTENTS

PART I
THE PHILOSOPHY OF DEBT AVOIDANCE / 1

PART II
CREDITORS SUE DEBTORS:
THE DEBTOR ON THE DEFENSE / 71

PART III
DEBTORS SUE CREDITORS: DEBTORS ON THE OFFENSE / 121

DEDICATION

This book is dedicated to my mother Effie, the most wonderful mother in the world; to my triplets: Lukas, Geli, and Carmen Effie, who were born on June 24, 2002, during the writing of this book; to my wife Rocky, who made the wonderful triplets and the book possible; and to Stavros Stavrikos, Mavriki, and Rodniki, for their indefatigable support and encouragement.

ACKNOWLEDGMENTS

I wish to express my sincere appreciation to the following people whose immensely important contribution to this book made it possible: Jill Alexander, my editor at Adams Media; Peter Miller of PMA literary agency, my literary lion agent who never gives up; James Chaffee, my amanuensis extraordinaire; E.G. for always being there for me; and last but not least, Sir Isaac Newton, Albert Einstein, Werner Heisenberg, and all those other famous physicists whose "laws of physics" expressed a fundamental truth about our world, and whose immutable laws have been transmuted in this book into "laws of the law."

PART I

THE PHILOSOPHY
OF DEBT
AVOIDANCE

1

"BEING STRONG MEANS NEVER HAVING TO SAY YOU'RE SORRY"

FROM THE DAY they crawl out of their cradles, Americans are relentlessly taught the value of "paying one's debts." Yet in today's world, what is truly a "legitimate debt" is often a matter of perception, cagey legal strategy, and ever-changing laws and mores.

Every year, millions of American individuals and businesses succumb to the stentorian demands of creditors and collection agencies, throw in the towel, and sell or give up their homes, cars, and credit cards by filing for bankruptcy. Many accept creditors' judgment of themselves as "failures," and they allow their problems to bring them to the point of deep depression or even suicide.

The real secret, however, is that bankruptcy (not to mention suicide) is rarely the best option available. Bankruptcy does not dispose of IRS tax obligations or student loan debts, and it creates a stigma that will damage the debtor for many years to come. As for depression and suicide, they are demons to be exorcised, not solutions to be embraced. No mere debt or financial problem is worth the ruin of a single debtor's life.

If bankruptcy and depression still carry stigmas because they are an admission of personal failure, debt litigation is the very opposite: a manifestation of personal success, clever tactics, and newly discovered self-empowerment.

Psychologists tell us that mental depression stems from feeling helpless and from directing outward aggression toward oneself. Small wonder, then, that the more debt people pile on their backs, the more helpless and depressed they feel. It is not mere coincidence that the recent explosion in sales of antidepressant drugs, psychiatric hours chalked up, and mental anguish have been riding side by side with the cavalcade of debt that now dominates the consumer economy.

There is no better way to regain your self-esteem and self-confidence than to "sock it" to one or more of your creditors. Beating back and lashing out at your creditors not only gives you a reinvigorated feeling of accomplishment and control of your personal destiny, it also literally improves your finances by allowing you to pursue a strategy of "selective debt payment." This strategy allows you to choose those few creditors whom you wish to pay regularly, in order to preserve continuing "good credit" with them, while pursuing the policy of debt avoidance with other creditors who have violated some rule of law or ethical maxim.

It is indeed an interesting phenomenon, verified by psychologists, that people are generally conditioned to feel "guilty" if they do not pay their debts on time. This feeling of massive guilt is exploited by creditors and collection agencies, who will resort to any tactic—no matter how harassing or unethical—to squeeze the last dime out of a debt-and-guilt-plagued consumer.

But who are these creditors, anyway, who make us feel so guilty about not paying them? Is it really right for a gargantuan corporation like Bank of America to charge an arbitrary and exorbitant "late fee" whenever your monthly payment arrives a day late? Is this legal? Does the application of late fees and other dubious charges to your credit account entitle you to a moratorium on paying your debts to the bank? Should it? Does a creditor like AT&T Wireless have the right to arbitrarily tack on surcharges and "new" charges any time it feels like it?

As the economy has continued to deteriorate in the miasma of the Bush Depression, more and more creditors have turned to the tactic of adding on hidden surcharges for services you had originally contracted for free. This trick has been a source of revenue for the creditors to combat the tough times. Many airlines have begun charging customers up to $100 for standby, despite no agreement by the consumer to pay this; phone companies have quadrupled their fees for minimal services such as directory assistance; and so forth.

Each of these unilaterally imposed surcharges form a basis for the debtor to dispute his entire statement or credit card bill. Any such change, imposed without your consent, is per se illegal and constitutes a basis for a fraud and breach of contract suit against the creditor.

But, in order to enforce your rights and "stand up" to the Enrons and AT&Ts of this world, you need an arsenal of weapons.

Much of this book is about how to hone and use one's legal swords and shields in the courtrooms of America, and how to mount wars of attrition against overreaching creditors. But the questions we ask in this chapter are: "Is such a strategy morally right? Is it ethical? Is it just and fair?"

THE QUESTIONABLE ETHICS
OF MONEYLENDING

Western civilization has always had an ambivalent attitude toward money, and toward the debt collection system that enforces the world of moneylending. On the one hand, we all worship the almighty dollar and wish we could become millionaires, either by winning the lottery or by hitting the big time through a magical stroke of luck. Americans, in particular, worship the Golden Calf of Money, and even many preachers shout from their pulpits that one's materialistic success in life is a measure of one's status as a member of "the elect of God."

On the other hand, Americans' worship of money has uneasily existed side by side with a deeply felt skepticism about money, its corrupting power, and the spiritual emptiness of a life spent in the pursuit of materialistic gain. "What shall it profit a man," asks Jesus, "if he should gain the whole world and lose his own soul?"

Those haunting words create a cognitive dissonance in our attitude toward money. We like to see millionaires and celebrities humiliated through scandal and bad publicity. Our scandal-mongering, shallow press is always on the lookout for a fabulously rich person brought down by his or her own greed. Though we may not like to admit it, a part of us likes to see rich people and companies fail, because in each of those scandals we share a secret but mighty triumph. If this is so, why should we cringe with guilt at the thought of not paying a creditor on some alleged debt?

Why, indeed.

Of course, there is no clear answer to this question. For each person who pursues the unbeaten path of debt avoidance, this question can only be answered by looking into one's own soul. Each of us must balance his or her conscience with one's goals in life and the tools created in society to give us what we want.

Any judge and litigator will tell you, "What is legal is not necessarily what is just." As the legendary Chicago attorney Clarence Darrow put it nearly a century ago, "True justice is for angels, not for men."

In this type of an imperfect world, how can creditors insist upon absolute and unconditional payment of debts? How can they be so sure they are "right" in some legalistic, or moral, sense?

So, whenever you face the inevitable existential question, "To Pay or Not to Pay," you should think of these things and then make your decision. Let no one else make the decision for you.

AMERICA: LAND OF THE FREE, HOME OF THE DEBTOR

The United States today is the greatest debtor nation in the history of the world. Apart from the "national debt," which is owed by the government to "investors" foreign and domestic, the total amount of consumer debt is truly staggering. As of 2002, the total amount of consumer debt in this country exceeds $1.7 trillion. This amounts to an average consumer debt of $121,000 per adult, which will take an average of fifty years to pay off. Two-thirds of all sales in the annual U.S. economy are sales based on debt. Indeed, consumer debt is the "engine" which drives our economy. Without consumer debt, our economy would come to a standstill.

What is the meaning and nature of debt? Debt is, literally, a means of financing the purchase of durable goods and services that are far beyond our means and self-discipline. By signing up to borrow money to purchase these items and services, the consumer is voluntarily placing himself into slavery; he is "legally bound" to pay off the lender, no matter how long it takes, no matter how many times the original debt has been multiplied by usury.

What is it about human nature that makes debt a perpetual plague? Why can't people learn to live within their means, to heed the admonitions of the Bible and the wise words of Ben Franklin's *Poor Richard's Almanac?*

Today, thanks to the enormously liberal lending practices of creditors, a man on a $100,000 salary can easily slip on the mantle of a millionaire by buying a million-dollar mansion, a Mercedes, and a series of luxury goods—all on credit. This illusion can seem quite real—that is, until Joe Debtor loses his job during an economic downturn and watches his million-dollar house of cards collapse into a pile of debt.

Indeed, living beyond one's means has become the prevailing modus operandi for Americans. Today, few can afford to pay for what they purchase.

The corollary of the twisted value system of our Great Debtor Age is that being a debt slave is a good thing because it forces us to yield to an external form of "discipline" when we cannot impose discipline on ourselves.

But wait a minute! Can this mentality really make sense? When a society chooses slavery because it admits that it cannot police itself, isn't that society in great trouble?

Apparently, Americans don't think this is anything to worry about.

"JUST SAY NO" TO YOUR CREDITORS

But does the modern American debt slave really have to fulfill his contract with the creditor devil? What would happen if debtor-slaves began to revolt *en masse*? Would the system shut down if debtors defaulted on a mass scale? Who would be around to "collect the uncollectable"?

Well, the fact is that debtors *can* "just say no" to their creditors, and the purpose of this book is to show them how.

Young Hamlet can and will indeed confront that eternal question, "To Pay or Not to Pay?" and he will be shown how to "Just Say No," but in a different sense than is commonly thought.

Interestingly, it was the wife of one of the most notorious debtors of all time, Ronald Reagan, who gave us the immortal line that is every debtor's lifeline to survival. At the same time that Reagan charted a course that landed the country in huge debts, with multi-billion dollar annual deficits and multi-trillion dollar national debts, his wife, Nancy, was also telling us, "Just Say No."

Every debtor in this country should take up this mantra— literally.

IS THERE LIFE AFTER A CREDIT MELTDOWN?

One of the main reasons why debtors prostrate themselves before creditors, and pay up even the most disputed claims, is the fear of "credit meltdown."

The dreaded "credit reporting bureaus" are powerful enough to strike fear into even the most hardy and courageous of debtors. Their credit "rating" number or letter rank can literally mean life or death to millions in this Great Debtor Age. "I value my good credit as I value my good name!" goes the slogan. To be scarred with a "bad credit history" in this society, according to popular myth, is to forever cut oneself off from the Good Life available with unlimited future credit and to be stigmatized as a deadbeat, a bum, a lowlife, an insect.

Polls show that one of Americans' very worst fears, right behind getting killed or having to give a public speech before an audience, is that of having "bad credit." Credit reporting bureaus, like Equifax, Experian, TransUnion, and a host of less well-known acronyms, strike terror in the hearts of all average consumers.

It is perhaps this fear of getting "bad credit," more than anything else, that impels debtors to fall into line and pay up no matter how unfair the charge, no matter how onerous the burden.

It is true that in today's computerized world, having bad credit is a severe handicap. Today, employers and prospective employers, landlords, mortgage companies, and everyone who is anyone tends to look up a consumer's credit rating before saying yea or nay to a job, an apartment, a loan, or even the most essential goods or services.

In the old days—which is to say, up until this century—the debtor's stigma was literally translated into debtor's prisons, where those who failed to pay their debts were literally thrown into jails and kept there until the debt was paid.

Today, the functional equivalent of the debtor's prison is the credit reporting bureau. The only difference is that instead of losing one's liberty, one now loses his or her reputation and right to obtain goods and services deemed essential. A bad credit rap sheet can be even more detrimental to life and limb than an actual criminal record, because you can't play the game of life if businesses won't sell to you on credit. In general, credit defaults and delinquencies now are reported on computers over the Internet, and they become part of a person's credit rating worldwide in an instant.

Another adjunct of the credit reporting bureaus, called the "credit rating agency," gives a person a credit rating, a FICO number from 0 to 1000. Many probably wonder if there is really any way to get around a bad credit rating, to appeal it, or to have it removed.

In reality, all those myriad "debt repair" scams offer no real solution to this dilemma. In general, these outfits offer just a chimera for sale, either something outright illegal (such as changing one's Social Security number) or something utterly facetious (such as writing Shakespearean prose to the credit reporting bureaus to clean up one's record).

CREDIT REPORTING BUREAUS: THE KAFKA'S CASTLE OF CREDIT

In general, credit reporting bureaus (CRBs) are Kafkaesque institutions—aloof, faceless, and unapproachable. They are run by armies of nondescript computers and faceless bureaucrats whom you never see and never talk to, but who hold the power to destroy your ability to live. Many CRBs have no one available to discuss problems with debtors on the phone. Calls to the agencies result in interminable tape recordings directing the debtor to "write in" any credit disputes.

But the Kafkaesque facade is just that—a facade. Credit reporting bureaus are like any other entity, and they follow the inexorable laws of credit law and economics.

To sue them, it is only necessary to have the right equipment, and the right mentality. The debtor must be prepared for total war, and in total war, anything goes, anything is fair game.

One difference between credit bureaus and ordinary creditors is the cause of action or legal theory under which one can sue the faceless credit reporting bureaus. Because they are not creditors themselves, but rather just credit reporting agencies, they cannot be sued for breach of contract, etc.

Rather, the key weapon to be used against credit reporting bureaus is the credit defamation cause of action.

Whenever a credit reporting bureau reports and publishes and broadcasts information about a consumer, it is liable for defamation. This can be the wedge the consumer needs to use the laws of economic reality against the credit reporting bureaus.

COLLECTION AGENCIES: THE 800-POUND GORILLAS IN THE RING

COLLECTION AGENCIES ARE the shock troops of creditors. In many respects, they are the front-line soldiers in the creditor debtor wars, and in 97 percent of all cases they roll over the lonely and defenseless debtor like a Sherman tank over a lowly snail trying to cross the road. The collection agencies, well aware of this fact, act as if they were officially sanctioned, infallible entities acting with the imprimatur of Almighty God, instead of as what they truly are: petty, morally dubious, and ruthless businesses that thrive by harassing and threatening debtors into submission. As such, they operate on often shaky legal and ethical grounds, and can be brought to account for over-reaching by being sued and countersued for violation of fair debt collection laws, both state and federal. Though many debtors and consumers don't know it, most collection agencies break the law *on a routine basis* and can therefore be tripped up and brought to their knees by the clever consumer. Because there exist strict legal limits to what they can do to consumers, there are severe legal penalties hanging over their heads at all times.

THE TYPICAL COLLECTION SCENARIO

Most often, a credit card bank or company will first threaten the
debtor with the horror of being "sent to collections." After two
or three months of delinquency, on average, accounts are sent
to collection agencies, which then assume title to the credit and
inform the debtor, in no uncertain terms, that unless the money
is paid immediately, and in full, dire consequences will follow.

In most cases of the law, threatening someone with dire
consequences in order to extract money is a felony known as
"extortion." But because the laws are written by legislators who
are in the pockets of creditors, debt collection is exempted
from this rule. Yet the exemption is not absolute; there are still
some laws that protect debtors. Those laws are on the books to
be used, and it is a foolish debtor who fails to take advantage
of them.

Anyone who has been delinquent or sent to collections
knows the routine campaign: endless harassing phone calls, followed by a rapid-fire barrage of letters and other assaults aimed
at scaring the debtor into ponying up the amount of the debt
currently due.

WHAT TO DO WHEN COLLECTORS
STEP OVER THE LINE

What most people do not know is that virtually all states—and
the federal government—have "consumer protection" laws that
forbid collection agencies and their progeny from engaging in
"harassing" debt collection activity. Most states have a "fair debt
collection practices act" ("FDCPA"), which is an extremely powerful weapon for the debtor to have in his arsenal. These laws
entitle the debtor to sue the creditor (or to countersue him) in
court if the creditor uses annoying or improper debt collection
tactics. Examples are: telephoning the debtor so many times as

to constitute harassment, reporting the debtor as a deadbeat to third parties and employers, contacting a debtor's family members, and so on.

As a practical matter, most collection agencies and creditors routinely violate the FDCPA nearly every day. There is often no written record of the number of times the bad guys phone a debtor, but this can be uncovered during the "discovery" phase of the lawsuit. The debtor can rely on his memory to estimate the specific times, but it would be a very good idea to keep a journal near the phone and to record each harassing and annoying call. Such evidence, called "contemporaneous" in legalese, can be used in court and is a powerful weapon. If the collector is local and makes harassing calls from across the debtor's city, there is often no way to prove these calls, because most phone companies do not keep a record of local calls. If the call is made long distance or through an 800 number, it is easier to trace.

WHAT IS "HARASSMENT"?

What constitutes "harassing" activity—in particular, for purposes of the FDCPA? As with 99 percent of all issues before the law, this question is hopelessly ambiguous. Harassment is in the eye of the beholder. The very same behavior that is harassing to one person can be considered neutral or even favorable to another. This is indeed a solipsistic issue, and it can be easily exploited in the chaotic atmosphere of court, to the debtor's benefit. The more eyewitnesses the debtor has to the harassment, the better off he is; each witness is a bullet in the war against debt collectors. Debtors should round up as many friends, colleagues, family members, and others who can testify as to the effect of the collection harassment on the debtor. "I saw Sally burst into tears" . . . "My friend fell apart and went bonkers after receiving a call from the collection agency" . . .

"Jim just went ballistic and could not work for three days after getting the call."

Following what we can call "Einstein's Theory of Legal Relativity" ("What one perceives as 'truth' is relative to one's frame of reference, and not absolute, in every sense"), every allegation is relative in the law. What is harassment to debtor "A" may not seem like harassment to debtor "B."

More importantly, Einstein's Theory of Legal Relativity means that when the case gets to a jury, it is impossible to predict how the jury will vote: yea or nay on harassment. Creditors' lawyers know this: No matter how much a creditor-lawyer may boast and bluster about how he is "going to win this slam-dunk case," he knows damn well that a jury verdict cannot be predicted. As any trial lawyer or judge will tell you, a trial is always a "crapshoot." The role of whimsy, caprice, prejudice, and outright emotion cannot be overestimated when it comes to a jury. Manipulating the minds of twelve people is quite easy. By appealing to the emotion of the jury, a debtor can often get away with murder (legally, of course). If the jury feels sorry for a debtor, and hates an unpopular creditor, it will vote for the debtor. That is a fact that you can take to the bank.

THE PRE-EMPTIVE STRIKE OF CREDIT PROTECTION

To defeat your creditor opponent, you must adopt a jujitsu strategy of using his own heavy-handed tactics against him; force must be turned around and aimed at the creditor. When the creditor goes too far in seeking to collect a debt, such as by harassing the debtor no end, he is unwittingly handing the debtor the rope by which to hang the creditor himself.

I had a case once in which a seventy-nine-year-old lady (the perfect debtor-litigant, made to order) faced foreclosure on her house because the mortgage company declared her in default (no payments made in ninety days). We sued the bad guys first, thus launching a "pre-emptive strike" against them and forcing them to confront the reality of what they were up against. They wound up reducing the debt by 10 percent, shaved off massive (usurious) interest, and forgot about foreclosure. In general, no creditor will risk a nasty and expensive legal war against an "Aunt Mathilda" type of debtor, because such a sympathetic debtor will always appeal to a jury.

Such sympathetic witnesses serve as powerful fodder for the FDCPA machine in court. An even better eyewitness is a doctor, an expert witness who can testify as to the effect of debt collection activity on his debtor-patient. "Leon suffers from post-traumatic stress disorder, and this debt collection harassment set him back five years in his therapy . . . ." Such a statement, coming from the mouth of a certified M.D. with a credible practice, is worth thousands of dollars in court. If the debtor can show the creditor that he has medical records proving his emotional distress, the collector may go away. At the very least, the debt should be reduced substantially if not forgiven altogether.

TURNING THE TABLES ON DEBT COLLECTION: GOING TO TRIAL

According to what we will call the "Reno-Hollywood Law of Jury Trials," verdicts are utterly arbitrary and are usually based on: (1) luck or chance; and (2) the histrionic talents of the players.

Einstein's Theory of Legal Relativity provides great weapons in the hands of an astute debtor. This is necessarily so because the corollary of Einstein's theorem is that a debtor can employ "legal jujitsu" and turn collection activities around on the creditors and their collection agencies, flip-flopping the 800-pound gorillas and landing them flat on their backs.

Just a few hours spent studying the appropriate consumer protection laws will enable the debtor to sue the collection agency and its parent controller, the original creditor, for violation of the Fair Debt Collection Practices Acts.

In most states, statutes provide for large and sometimes triple damages for a collection agency's violation of the anti-harassment statutes. In addition, attorney fees are usually awarded to a prevailing debtor who sues under these statutes.

Once the lawsuit is filed, the 800-pound gorilla is stunned and lying flat on his back, wondering what to do next. But flipping the gorilla around isn't enough. In addition to attacking the collection agencies, the wise and prudent debtor will also reach out and strike at the original creditor (the credit card issuer, bank, or merchant) by naming it as a co-defendant in the lawsuit, as well as individual collectors, harassing callers, and the like. In general, following the principle of "the more the merrier," the wise debtor will bring in as many individual defendants as possible, linking them all to the abusive "harassing" practice of the collection agency. One advantage of maximizing the number of defendants is that for each defendant named, the costs to each of your opponents increase tenfold. I call this the "law of exponential cost growth."

For each defendant named in a suit, the debtor-plaintiff is entitled to send out a massive barrage of questions ("interrogatories") in legal form designed to uncover the activities of the other side. This barrage of questions is called "discovery." Each time one of the defendants faces the need to respond to this massive discovery in his own right his costs increase tenfold, on average. The numerous types of discovery fall into different legal categories. There are interrogatories, requests for document production, subpoenas, depositions, and requests for admission. This does not even get into the area of experts. There are identification of experts, deposition of experts, and requests for inspection so that experts can examine physical evidence. All of this becomes expensive, at times very expensive.

Why? First of all, the scavengers of the collection trade, "debt collection attorneys," will quickly drop by the wayside. The typical collection attorney "firm" generally operates as a mass-production assembly-line "default factory." Like vultures, they generally take cases on contingency for a percentage of the money collected. This is the same premise under which the collection agencies themselves are operating.

The collection agency attorneys operate primarily on the scare tactic of the attorney-lawsuit threat. As soon as that fails to achieve results, they are already operating outside of the range of their profit margin or legal experience. As a general rule, they rake off 20 to 50 percent of whatever they collect, and they do not charge creditors or collection agencies by the hour. This presumes that all they have to do for their money is to file and serve suit on the debtor, rolling over the prostrate debtor to an easy "default" and then levying his assets. These firms are just not equipped to handle heavy-duty litigation such as that of debt collection harassment suits. They don't have the manpower, the time, or the expertise to get bogged down in such a quagmire.

Thus, every time the collection lawyers encounter a "live wire" debtor, one who dares to "Just Say No," they generally hand back the case to the collection agency or creditor, who then has to find a "real" litigation firm to defend against the suit. Ten thousand dollars is the typical minimum retainer required as a minimum by any reputable litigation firm to handle such a case. What this means is, if your debt is less than a minimum amount, you will probably be written off as a bad debt and left alone. The creditor will probably settle the case with you either for free, or for pennies on the dollar.

As a general rule, the prudent debtor should never offer to settle for more than ten cents on the dollar. Unless there is some hidden agenda or extraneous factors operating, it is tom-foolery to pay more than a dime on the dollar, because of the underlying economics of litigation involved. As will be shown later in the uses of discovery, it is fairly easy to batter down the ramparts of collectors with these tactics. Results can be expected in three to six months. The creditor will cry "Uncle," as surely as the sun will rise from the east tomorrow morning. The laws of litigation economics cannot be ignored and they always work in favor of the debtor.

A not atypical example is the recent case of a daughter, who we will call Dorothy, whose mother was also named Dorothy. As Dorothy II, the daughter, was using her maiden name for purposes of credit, the two women had the same first and last name. A mindless collection agency, acting on behalf of a behemoth retailer that shall remain nameless, made the mistake of phoning and writing letters to the debtor's parents, Dorothy I and her husband, calling them every day. This created an intolerable situation of harassment for the mother who had no relationship with the debt or the collection agency coming after her. When the legal dust settled, the claims of the mother far outweighed the value of the daughter's debt, and a settlement was reached rather easily.

The point is that the wrongful actions of the collection agency is a bargaining chip that can be put to use in myriad creative ways.

3

CREDIT REPAIR SCAMS:
THE SNAKE OIL SALESMEN
OF OUR TIME

THE SOLICITATIONS FOR credit repair are persistent and ubiquitous. Anyone remotely familiar with e-mail, unsolicited advertisements on the Internet, and junk mail knows that there seem to be an unlimited number of faceless companies and persons out there claiming to have a "magic formula" for cleaning up a person's credit in an instant.

Such credit repair entities offer magic bullets to wipe out the bad credit monster: from about $50 for an Internet packet of useless material "guaranteed" to repair credit "in three minutes" or "two weeks," to thousands of dollars for elaborate "seminars" with a "credit professional," and the like.

The credit repair scams ("CRS") are the snake oil salesmen of our time. Like their Wild West predecessors, they blow into town announcing that they have the miracle cure for a malady, soak up the cash, then depart before any victim knows whatever happened. Also, like their frontier counterparts, they generally buttress their credibility by proffering "witness testimonials." In the modern version, a seemingly "independent" customer stands before the camera or the computer screen and recites a carefully scripted testimonial about how great the CRS product has been for him.

The testimonials are generally uttered by shills, confederates in the pay of the CRS scam-artist. They generally use fake names and often cannot be traced. Many times the names sound genuinely authentic and credible, using hackneyed but credible terms such as "Fidelity," "Trust," "National," "American," etc.

Because credit repair scams are not considered a legitimate "profession" and are not licensed by any government entity, they have no accountability. These latter-day snake oil salesmen can soak up millions of dollars in fees, then close down shop and disappear, or file for bankruptcy, or otherwise abscond with the cash.

Though they generally offer "cash back guarantees," these "guarantees" are generally unenforceable and worthless, are not honored by the CRS peddlers, and have trick escape clauses of all sorts of ambiguous words in small lettering. This enables them to get out of the refund guarantee by claiming that the customer "used our service" and thereby received a quid pro quo for his money.

In almost every case of the CRS hucksters, there is a mass of advertising propaganda aimed at promising the unfortunate debtor the world and the moon and stars, followed by a few sketchy details. Phrases like "instant credit," "guarantees," and so on are sprinkled around the solicitations like sugar in cereal.

THE LINCOLN PENNY SCAM

The CRS companies closely resemble a scam that was finally put down by the government in the 1950s (after millions were robbed). This "Lincoln Penny Portrait" scam placed ads in numerous magazines and newspapers, promising to mail customers "an authentic original portrait of Abraham Lincoln" if they sent in $100. Promising that the portrait would be "worth more in the future," the scam artists attracted millions of suckers, took their money, then mailed them a bright and shiny Lincoln penny, worth exactly one cent. Claims of fraud were dismissed with the words, "It *is* an original portrait."

Similarly, CRS scams operate in much the same way. After the debtor has signed up for their service and has sent in his check or credit card payment, one of two things will happen. Either he'll receive a password for entry into a Web site, where he's offered a few words of meaningless babble, or he gets a letter or brochure in the mail telling him that all of his bad credit ratings can be wiped out if he pays all his outstanding debts. Or, in the alternative, he is advised to write to credit reporting bureaus demanding that they prove that he actually made all of the charges or remove the bad credit rating from the reports.

Such scams claim to be "legit" and nonfraudulent, because in a technical sense they literally do what they promise to do: A Lincoln penny is, technically, a portrait of Lincoln, just as the advice to pay off debt and contact credit agencies is, technically, true. Credit reporting agencies are supposed to remove the negative credit reports if the merchant does not provide proof of charges, but as a practical matter, this is a hit-and-miss affair and the merchants usually do provide proof within the sixty days normally allowed for disputing a debt. Since most debts are more than sixty days old, this gambit is usually pointless and does not clear up the debtor's records in any way, shape, or form.

Even if one chose to go after these CRS operators for fraud—civil or criminal fraud—one would get nowhere. In general, no prosecutor or judge would waste his time bringing them to account, and would instead revert to the maxim, *De Minimis Non Curat Lex* ("The law does not concern itself with trifles").

In addition to being amorphous and unaccountable, these fly-by-night outfits are generally short-lived, and go out of business after reeling in the loot from gullible debtors for a few months. Some of the CRS firms actually offer "credit consultants" and promise a full hour (or more) of "credit consultation," either on the phone or in person. The "consultants," however, are generally unqualified, lowly paid telemarketers who cannot do more than recite a script. They generally tell the debtor that they "cannot give legal advice" and refer all serious questions to an attorney. This is a clever ruse to avoid giving the customer a serious consultation: Most states ban any nonlawyer from "rendering legal advice." Since most credit consultations necessarily involve the rendering of legal advice, the hucksters have a loophole big enough to drive a tank through—and, again, they are "technically" correct.

The truth is that CRS is a bogus business with nothing of any value to offer debtors, except illusions of deliverance and temporary relief from the Big Bad Wolf.

THE BORN-AGAIN SCAM

There are a number of scams in the "too good to be true" category of painless credit repair. One of the most ruthless is the promise that "you as a debtor" can easily and painlessly sweep the plate clean, start from scratch, and wipe out all of your debts (and negative credit reports) in one fell swoop. These operators simply inform their customers that their credit records are based on their Social Security numbers. In doing so they state (or more often merely strongly imply) that if the debtor can simply change his or her Social Security number ("SSN"), he will be "born again" as a new debtless consumer. Therefore, on applying for credit, and subsequently obtaining new credit cards under an imaginary or pirated Social Security number belonging to someone else, the debtor will be home free with a newly blank slate in regard to credit.

This born-again credit repair scam is actually illegal and constitutes a federal felony (e.g., using someone else's SSN, or inventing one). However, because trafficking in fake or pirated SSNs is a big business in this country, and because the Social Security Administration is miles behind the SSN roadrunners, the scheme is appealing to desperate debtors, who can later claim they made a "mistake" if caught.

The truth is that in our computer-cyberspace age, all of a person's debts are inexorably tied to his or her name, address, job, telephone number, and a whole host of other identifiers, as well as to that SSN. If caught, a debtor using a fake SSN will have very likely added criminal charges to his list of problems without affecting the accumulated debts by even one cent.

Ironically, the fake SSN scam is probably the only effective (albeit illegal) remedy for bad credit, among the repertoire of fake cures offered by the CRS pushers. At least, if you get away with it, you really and truly can become born again with a new identity—unless (or it should be said, until) you get caught. For some people with little left to lose, and a whole lot of desperation, the risk might be worth taking. But that is not advice that should be given to anyone as a practical matter. The fact that there may be persons who are that desperate is another problem in our society that we can only deplore.

For the high rollers among the debtor gamblers, those willing to risk prison in order to get out of debt, some of the more sleazy credit hucksters actually offer their customers the SSN of a dead or living person who has or had an excellent credit rating. Coupled with this gambit, there is usually a recommendation for the debtor to take on the name of the defunct debtor, thus assuming a new identity and adding another felony to his list of crimes. Taking over another person's identity is, of course, a crime, and a much sleazier crime than just making up an SSN cold turkey. In the instance of identity theft, a real person and his heirs can be harmed by this crime and will suffer the damaging effects through no fault of his own.

In the modern age, when computers hold such a vast storage of information about millions of people, it is relatively easy for any merchant or investigator to tap into a computer and "find" a Social Security number belonging to a debtor with A-1 credit, or having no credit record at all. The bottom line is that the only way to clean up one's bad credit, in the "born again" scenario, is to commit felonies and hope not to get caught.

THE SHAKESPEARE'S GHOST SCAM

Of the various types of credit repair scam outfits, the one that comes closest to offering something legitimate for the money raked in is dubbed "Shakespeare's ghost." Ultimately, though, this "credit repair" solution has next to no effect, and the credit rating of the unsuspecting victim ends up just as bad, if not worse, than it was before.

The Shakespeare's ghost scam artists among us tell their suckers that if they just pony up a few thousand dollars up front, they will receive a folio manuscript from their master writers. This manuscript can be duly dispatched to credit reporting agencies and creditors and will prove that "the pen is mightier than the dollar."

These Shakespearean CRS agents purport to have some "inside knowledge" of how to write to the bureaus and creditors, but in fact this knowledge is something the debtor can discover himself with a short trip to the law library. For credit card debts, there are federal (and some state) laws requiring credit reporting agencies to remove negative credit information from a consumer's records if the consumer, or his representatives (such as the Shakespeare CRS), writes letters disputing the debts.

Since most merchants and credit agencies will have no problem in proving the validity of the debt (i.e., that the debtor signed on the dotted line and received some good or service in return), it follows that Shakespeare winds up empty-handed at least 98 percent of the time.

But the debtors foolish enough to hire the Shakespeares would be better off saving their money and doing a little research themselves, to see how they could write to creditors to dispute debts. Why hire someone else to do what you can do yourself in five minutes?

In those few instances where debtors figure this out and themselves write long letters to their creditors asking for proof of debt, the transactions (at best) will be tied up in temporary ad hoc disputes. Then they will be plastered back onto the credit report as soon as the merchant responds. These victims are told that if they write to each credit card company or other creditor, and demand to dispute each and every transaction on their credit histories, the companies must respond within sixty days or else the credit bureaus must remove all such delinquent records from the debtor's files. As a practical matter, while there are consumer laws on the books actually requiring creditors to verify all disputed debts, these laws generally limit the amount of time for demanding a recount to sixty days from date of purchase. In addition, the three major credit reporting agencies in the country (Equifax, Experian, and Trans-Union) generally totally ignore the debt-discounting letters and refuse to remove any negative credit remarks on their reports. This is a fact that credit cleanup scams often fail to tell their customers.

What happens is that for a small fortune, which would be much better spent elsewhere (such as suing creditors or paying bills), the debtor hires the Shakespeare clone to write meaningless form letters that are highly unlikely to produce any useful results. Even if the debts for the past sixty days are temporarily removed from the reports, those older than sixty days will remain for years.

After letters, whether written by Shakespeare or by the debtor himself, are routinely ignored and trashed by the credit reporting agencies, credit card companies, and banks and creditors, it is the debtor who is left holding an empty bag. He is far more likely to wind up in collections than to get a response. To force the credit reporters to remove the negative information from the report, the debtor must sue them in court.

THE REALITY OF CREDIT REPAIR

The reality is that there is no legitimate way to clean up bad credit, short of suing the creditors and forcing them to negotiate a deal, including removal of credit libel from your rap sheet, and that every outfit that offers a magic solution is a fraud and a scam. But because people will forever grasp at straws when sold on an illusion through clever advertising propaganda and a drumbeat marketing campaign, there will be more than enough suckers to fatten the wallets of these con artists.

Because most Americans were raised on the "ethical" principle that one should always pay one's bills on time, they feel guilty about stiffing creditors and even guiltier about having bad credit. This makes them all the more susceptible to credit repair scams, because they experience "psychic dissonance," an uncomfortable feeling of tension resulting from the contradiction between their ideals (honest debtor) and their reality (deadbeat debtor).

Thus, the credit repair scams are based on clever and cynical psychological manipulation of debtors. These operators know that desperate debtors will grasp at straws and thereby believe that they can magically clean up their credit by paying money to some faceless outfit for the secret formula.

FOR DEBTOR LEMMINGS:
THE DEBT CONSOLIDATION SCAM

While the debt "repair" scams are among the sleaziest and least effective out there, the debt "consolidation" services offer a little more bang for the buck, but not much more. Like their cousins, the CRSs, these outfits charge an arm and a leg to do for the debtor what he could easily do for himself.

While the CRS operations claim to have a magical formula and hidden inside information, debt consolidation scams claim to have "special relationships" with banks and other creditors, and promise that they can get the debtor "lower monthly payments," a lower interest rate, and a single monthly payment plan. They offer convenience and the illusion of reduced debt, but they too fall far short of what they promise to the unwary. At best, they can act as your debt-paying amanuensis, which will do nothing more than "consolidate" your debts by promising to arrange for "lower interest rates" and "one monthly payment"—while you pay them a very handsome fee for this minimal service.

While such a panacea seems tempting simply because it offers (1) convenience, (2) lower total monthly payments, and (3) lower interest rates, it comes at the cost of paying a middle man in the form of fees and a longer payoff period.

Though the debt consolidation outfits can actually come through with a lower total monthly payment and "consolidate" your debt, they more than make up for this by charging you a host of "administrative fees" and other costs that were never made clear up front. Moreover, turning over your bank records and finances to such debt consolidation outfits is very risky business. The amount of sheer theft, embezzlement, and other forms of conversion practiced by these entities—many of which are fly-by-night operations who themselves disappear or go bankrupt after a few months—is truly staggering.

Apart from the inherently dubious nature of debt consoli-dation, the fact is that the debt consolidation outfits really have no effective way to convince banks and other creditors to lower interest rates or monthly payment schedules. Unless hav-ing to give up your credit charging privileges, getting your name forever blackened on credit reporting agencies' files as a "delinquent" debtor, paying extra administrative fees, and agreeing to roll in circles with a heavy millstone around your neck is considered a "service."

Some debt consolidation outfits engage in shaky (and ille-gal) Ponzi schemes. In this case, they rake in administrative fees first from Debtor A and later from Debtor B, then use the money from B to make a "payment" for A. Then it's on to Debtor C, until the cash runs out or is stolen by the principals. This is how they are able to "reduce" the amount of monthly payments debtors must make. Often, however, the debtor finds out too late that his entrusted debt agent has not paid the origi-nal creditors as promised, has closed up shop, and has escaped into the night. For this, there is no effective remedy.

The Ponzi scheme can last only up to a certain point: It is finite in time, and the debtor stands to lose money and wind up with egg on his face.

What if the debt consolidation service itself goes bankrupt or vanishes? What happens if you paid them, but they did not pay your underlying creditors?

Suing a bankrupt entity is strictly *verboten* in this country, and any suit filed against a bankrupt entity will be "stayed" and "frozen" by any civil court, pending bankruptcy resolution. Suing a vanished entity is virtually impossible. If the scoundrels have gobbled up the money and run, forget about going after them.

Debt consolidation agents are generally aggressive in snatching up the debtor's income sources. If you have a regular job with regular biweekly paychecks, the debt consolidation agent will generally insist that a very large portion of your income be directly deposited in the debt consolidation firm's account. What this means is that by the time someone brings the debtor the news that the debt consolidation firm is bankrupt, many months of the debtor's salary may have disappeared into the black hole of the debt consolidator's bank account.

And what about those merry "debt counselors" who offer you a "consultation"? The first consultation is generally free or requires a minimal deposit. Is there any risk of signing up in the long queue for debt counseling?

The question is, what is there to "counsel" about?

THE DEBT COUNSELOR: "GUILT, INC."

Debt "counselors" are generally the front men and women for debt consolidators and similarly unscrupulous scams. They tend to thrive on customers' guilt trips, by accusing the debtor of being guilty of "default" for starters, and then rounding him up for a "Jesus Talk."

As with the case of jailhouse lawyers, those scam-artists who make a living out of railroading the accused into quick plea bargains, debt counselors tend to make the debtor feel guilty about stiffing his creditors. "After all," they say, "didn't you use the poor creditor's generosity and loans to buy important items and services? So how can you not pay these kind and honorable debtors?"

After going through this "Jesus Talk," in which the debtor "confesses" his or her sins to the "counselor," the debtor is placed in a position of paying up huge fees to the counselor, all for being told he or she should feel guilty about owing the bad guys money (including usury). The debtor is then conned into setting aside a certain amount of money each month to pay the debt counselor a fee. Afterward, he is generally given a hodge-podge of useless information aimed at brainwashing him into paying his creditors in ample portions, even though they have already ruined his credit and shut off all his credit cards.

The fast-talking debt counselors, who are usually paid on commission for every sucker they reel in, recite a carefully rehearsed spiel promising the debtor the moon and the stars. This lures the debtor into committing to pay the counselors huge fees and to sign over his income to them. This high-pressure sales pitch strategy is designed to tempt desperate debtors into debt restructuring, debt consolidation, and similar schemes. It is only a year or two later when the debtor realizes that his money has gone into administrative fees and other overhead, and the reduced monthly interest payments were achieved with delayed balloon payments that are still due.

Again, debt counselors are generally ruthless fly-by-night organizations that employ an elaborate feeder system to lure debtors into their Ponzi schemes, and these outfits generally go bankrupt in a few months or, at best, years. The debtor only ends up further in debt, with his credit further damaged, and will likely face a disappeared or bankrupt outfit down the pike.

Why, you ask, doesn't Congress do something about these CRS operations, if they are so fraudulent?

Let's face the facts! Congress is in the hands of paid lobbyists for creditors and banks, which work hand-in-hand with the debt consolidation scam artists to fleece consumers. Add to this the "deregulation" mode we've been in over the past twenty years, and the political trend is to move away from regulating these scams, not toward it.

4

BANKRUPTCY: AN ILLUSORY
DEUS EX MACHINA FOR
DEBTORS

SO GREAT IS THE FEAR of Americans about bad debt that millions line up every year to seek "protection" from their creditors by filing for bankruptcy. Ironically, bankruptcy is the flip side of the credit genie illusion: Just as Joe Debtor once thought he could create instant wealth for free by rubbing a credit card genie, so too he thinks he can instantly escape his creditor wolves by rubbing the bankruptcy genie. In a society based on "instant gratification," bankruptcy does indeed seem like an "instant" solution to an unwieldy problem.

But what kind of solution is it, really?

Bankruptcy is initiated by filing a petition in a special federal bankruptcy court; this petition professes that a consumer is "insolvent" and therefore unable to pay his debts because his debts exceed his assets and income. Bankruptcy petitioners run to the "BK" court seeking protection from being committed to the equivalent of "debtors' prison."

The medieval paradigm was that individuals could be put into jail by their creditors for indeterminate sentences until they paid their bills. But, of course, they were never able to pay off their creditors because they were unable to earn money while in jail. This Middle Ages version of a Catch-22 did so much harm that modern societies developed a system of what was called "protection in bankruptcy" to stave off this calamity and restore people to a useful and productive life.

With a declaration that one is unable to pay his debts, one is presumed to have those debts forgiven and get a new lease on life. Unfortunately, nothing is ever that simple. As we have seen over and over, "unable to pay" is a highly relative term. Who wouldn't rather use his or her income from a particular month or year on a party for friends or to purchase a new car, and then claim to be unable to pay the bills that have accumulated in the same period of time? This is clearly not what was intended by the phrase "unable to pay." On the other hand, all of us would agree that a widow who is living on Social Security in a rented room is "unable to pay" the large debts that were incurred by her late husband's failed business. Almost everyone who is facing significant debt and might be considering seeking protection under the bankruptcy laws finds himself somewhere on a spectrum between those two extremes.

The issue that has to be decided is the amount of the sacrifice that should be made and the determination of the creditors. For most of the readers of this book, "can't pay" is a balancing act that involves keeping one's head above water using the information and understanding that we hope to convey in this book. Most of us can pay if we make the decision to pay at all costs. But the cost of that kind of sacrifice is often too great and, in the end, just not necessary.

Bankruptcy (or "BK" as it is called by lawyers) has increasingly become a way of life in the United States, after a history during which most people considered the thought of bankruptcy as the ultimate disgrace. Almost all of us either know, or have heard stories about, small business owners who worked hard for decades and devoted their lives to paying off debts that were incurred during or after the Crash of 1929 and the Great Depression, winding up in BK.

THE MODERN HISTORY OF BANKRUPTCY

The statistics tell the story of what has happened to the consumer credit industry in the United States. In the last year of World War II, there were 0.07 bankruptcies per 1,000 persons. By 1975 that figure had risen to 1.07 per 1,000 persons. That is an increase of slightly over 1,500 percent. After the implementation of the Federal Bankruptcy Law of 1978, there was a considerable increase and by 1987, there were 2.03 bankruptcies per 1,000 persons. Today, the figure is even greater, close to 4 bankruptcies per 1,000.

What is just as instructive is what has happened to the use of credit as a financial tool in this country. In 1945, when bankruptcies were rare, so was the total amount of consumer debt, which then amounted to 1.7 percent of a person's income, on average. By 1965 the ratio of debt to income had risen to 15.0 percent, an increase of nearly 900 percent. By 1987, the figure had skyrocketed to 19.3 percent of income, and today it approaches a staggering 30 percent.

The total amount of consumer credit card debt ("CCD") seems to double every ten years. According to the Nielson Report, the total amount of CCD in 1992 was $273.4 billion; in 2002, the figure doubled to over $550 billion. This massive increase in CCD has gone on unabated as the consumer's boat has yawed on the currents of red ink, and in the meantime, real disposable income has actually fallen or, at best, remained stagnant.

Anyone can see where this pattern is leading: more and more consumers unable to pay their creditors, more and more petitions for bankruptcy relief.

This massive increase in consumer debt has been rising in large part due to the massive increase in use of credit cards for consumer purchases. The country has come a long way from 1958, when Bank of America issued the first true credit card (then called "Bankamericard," later changed to "Visa"). The genius behind credit card issuance was that, in most people's minds, paying with plastic was functionally equivalent to getting something for free. Though payment could be deferred, interest could not be, but this was lost somewhere in the back of the consumer's mind.

When I was graduating from college in 1971, I was bombarded with dozens of offers for credit cards from banks, gasoline companies, and the like, despite the fact that I had no credit history and no source of income. Today, this strategy of "carpet-bombing" college students with credit cards, despite their having no means or record of paying these debts, continues unabated.

A twenty-one-year-old student with no income and no job is, in the minds of most mindless credit card issuers and "loan officers," a far better "credit risk" than a millionaire with a history of "bad credit." So blind and nearsighted is the credit industry to this fact, that a single credit dispute for $50 with a petty merchant, if reported on the millionaire's credit report, will *ipso facto* make the millionaire a worse credit risk than the unemployed student.

The original rationale for the carpet-bombing of credit applications on college students was that upon entering the marketplace college students would develop brand loyalty to the institutions that they first adopted and would enter retirement years later with the same credit cards and the same bank accounts. Of course, such a premise was soon shown to be groundless; most people follow the best deal at the time with no brand loyalty whatsoever.

In addition to blanketing students with credit card offers,

the credit industry has also sent out mass mailings to people on a random hit, with offers to "consolidate" their debts with one card, "low interest," and the like.

These relentless sales pitches, by making consumers feel comfortable with the concept of buying affluence with "magic plastic money," have turned this country truly into a Debtor's Nation. With average credit card interest hovering around 20 percent over the past thirty-seven years—far higher than the inflation rate and thus amounting to blatant usury—it is clear that the secret motive behind the credit card craze has been the desire to earn huge interest on this massive snowballing debt.

THE ILLUSION OF BANKRUPTCY PROTECTION

What is there to do when the debtor loses his job and source of income? Simple. File for bankruptcy.

Bankruptcy is, by far, the most alluring of the credit quick-fix remedies out there, for it offers the illusion of "starting over again," and it provides a quick Band-Aid to stop the bleeding of green blood. The minute the consumer files for BK, all creditors (except the IRS and school loans) must cease collection activity. Any lawsuit filed against a BK'd debtor must be stayed by the courts until the debtor has been discharged in the bankruptcy court, and the debtor usually walks away by paying pennies on the dollar.

Bankruptcy is a federal procedure, done in special federal "bankruptcy courts" that have sprouted up in every major city. Individuals seeking bankruptcy protection can file under either Chapter 7 or 13 of the federal bankruptcy code, while businesses must use Chapters 11 or 13. For a small court filing fee (usually $200 or less), one can immediately stop and freeze all lawsuits by creditors (again, except for the IRS and federally insured student loans). This initiates a moratorium period during which a trustee is appointed and a plan is worked out to climb out of the pit of BK, and work out a scheme for paying creditors pennies on the dollar.

Paying the minimal court fee is not the only cost of BK filing, of course. It is virtually de rigueur to hire a BK attorney to navigate the waters of this difficult and dangerous procedure. BK lawyers charge anywhere from a thousand dollars to hundreds of thousands, depending on the size of the estate and debt involved. Next, there are fees for the BK trustee, additional miscellaneous costs, tremendous opportunity costs, loss of property, and stigma.

In addition, in recent years, Congress has put more and more teeth into the criminal penalties for BK fraud. Under title 18 of the U.S. Code, section 152, BK fraud is presumed by law if the person filing for BK has made any luxury purchases or made cash advances totaling $1,000 or more within sixty days preceding the filing of the BK petition. And anyone caught hiding cash or other assets (by not declaring them on the endless forms) will be punished severely with a five-year prison sentence for each such concealment. Because BK fraud is a federal felony, and each such concealment constitutes a separate criminal count, with each count leading to a five-year prison sentence, one can see that seeking BK protection may well land a debtor in the slammer for the rest of his life.

Even if the BK'd debtor avoids prison, he can surely count on losing control of his life as well as many of his assets. The nightmare of having a trustee and other agents looking over one's shoulders for ten years is enough to drive even the most stalwart debtor batty, particularly with the threat of BK fraud hovering above his head like a sword of Damocles. If the BK'd debtor has more than one house, it will have to be turned over to the BK trustee to pay off the debts, as will multiple cars and certain "luxury" items.

There are four types of bankruptcy available to debtors

who feel they cannot pay their bills: Chapters 7, 11, 12, and 13 of the federal code. For most consumers (individuals) the commonly used bankruptcy chapter is "Chapter 7" of the federal code, though Chapter 13 may be a better remedy to avoid foreclosure on one's residence. Chapter 12 is available mainly for family farmers, and Chapters 11 and 13 are mainly used by company-debtors seeking protection from their creditors.

It is not uncommon to see individuals and couples, hitherto blessed with A-1 credit ratings and great jobs, dashing like lemmings into the illusory ocean of bankruptcy as a quick fix-all, just because their monthly payments have grown past what they expected. To say that this is ill-advised is an understatement.

Yet bankruptcy, like "credit repair" scams, offers but an illusion and delivers very little bang for the buck.

THE STIGMA OF BANKRUPTCY

Every four or five years, the wise lawgivers of Congress see fit to "tighten" the federal BK laws a little more, primarily to help out their corporate campaign contributors (i.e., the credit industry) by making it more difficult for individuals to qualify for BK protection. In 1994 and again in 1999, Congress passed "bankruptcy reform" laws that severely curtailed an individual's right to file for bankruptcy. The most recently proposed new "reforms" significantly tighten the requirements for individuals to file for bankruptcy and may end up vastly reducing the number of citizens who will be able to successfully file for BK. But it will not reduce the number of persons who think they need to file bankruptcy because they think they have no other choice to preserve their financial futures and protect their families.

Significantly, all of these BK "reform" laws are drafted and pushed through Congress by banking and credit card company lobbyists, such as those representing Bank of America, MBNA, and other major purveyors of credit cards. Not surprisingly, the reform laws do not tighten bankruptcy requirements for corporations, only for individuals seeking protection from hordes of creditors. And there is no compensating measure of relief to accompany the Draconian new laws: No caps on credit cards' usurious interest rates, no restrictions on deceptive marketing practices of banks and allied creditors who target the vulnerable and the desperate (such as young people with no credit history and no means of support), and no quid pro quo to compensate for taking away debtors' rights.

But assuming that one can qualify for bankruptcy protection, even under new Anti-Bankruptcy Laws, what benefits does this outlet really offer? Almost without exception, BK is virtually never the best course for a financially strapped individual or small business.

First, if an individual has been declared bankrupt, he or she must surrender all his credit cards. For at least seven years, he or she may be unable to qualify for any credit. If he or she has a home or car, these might be seized by the bankruptcy referee and the court. Almost certainly, second homes, cars, boats, and other "excess" goods will be seized and forfeited. Second, the debtor is forever stigmatized as a "deadbeat," for the stigma of bankruptcy goes a long way out to infinity. Anytime an individual applies for a new credit card, a home loan, a job, an apartment, or anything else, he or she will be asked, "Have you ever filed for bankruptcy?" If the answer is "Yes," the individual might as well forget about that loan or credit card—even after ten years have gone by. If you do somehow get a loan anyway, you can rest assured it will come out of the hands of a "hard money lender." This is a group of loan sharks who charge outrageous interest rates and other "administration costs" and who generally hedge their bets by requiring the posting of some kind of "collateral" for the loan. This "collateral" could come in the form of a lien against any property owned, a bank deposit as security, or some other sort of guarantee that has maximum impact on the individual's financial life in the event of a default.

Even after the ten-year "moratorium" for bankruptcy filing goes by, the stigma of bankruptcy will continue to follow the debtor for the rest of his life. Contrary to popular myth, the record of bankruptcy always exists somewhere on a debtor's computerized records and will rarely, if ever, be expunged. Anyone searching the records years from now can learn that a debtor filed for bankruptcy.

But the biggest surprise of all is that debtors can get all of the advantages of BK protection, without even filing for BK, by following the advice in this book to aggressively sue creditors. Suing a creditor, or countersuing him, will in effect get you the same, or better, relief as an expensive and dangerous BK filing, and you will not have to give up control of your life or your most prized possessions in the process. You will not need to wear the scarlet "BK" letter of shame for life, and you will be able to crawl out of the hole of debt.

The truth is that, by using the other chapters in this book, most debtors can pay some fraction of what they owe to get their debts cleared. At the same time, except for a handful of people who have a bitter former spouse or ex-business partner, few of us have creditors who will pursue us into bankruptcy. These are the few exceptional cases that prove the rule. Those are the cases that bankruptcy was really designed for, such as once-successful businessmen who were able to obtain huge unsecured loans and the holders of those notes who will wade through hell for their money. For those in a similar situation, the brief comments later in this book on asset protection will serve as an introduction to their future course, which should involve careful planning and a competent attorney.

Perhaps one of the saddest consequences of playing the

bankruptcy card is the devastating psychological effect that BK filing has on the debtor.

Many people become trapped in a hopeless mentality that offers no way out, save the disgrace of BK.

If at anytime you feel like there is no way out of debt but bankruptcy or suicide, don't jump—just sue the pants off of your creditors.

5

THE FUNGIBILITY OF MONEY
AND THE ECONOMICS OF
LITIGATION

YOU ARE NO DOUBT FAMILIAR with Copernicus, that great medieval scientist who proposed the radical concept that the earth and all the planets revolved around the sun, rather than vice versa.

What makes Copernicus significant here is how he turned the tables on the conventional wisdom of his time. Our understanding of the world is based on the concepts that we use to interpret it; what we need to do now is to turn the concepts of a system centered around creditors' desires on their proverbial heads and see the world through the eyes of a debtor.

Prior to Copernicus, everyone believed that the sun and planets revolved around the earth. The Catholic Church, in particular, found it necessary to regard the earth as the center of the universe in order to justify God's special concern for Man. (After all, why would God care a bit about petty Man if the earth were just a mote of dust floating around the Great Void?) But Nicolas Copernicus dared to defy this convention, and showed by complex mathematical equations that the conventional view could not be correct. He proposed the Heliocentric Theory, which has survived to the present day as a description of how the universe works and how the planets all circle the sun. In the world of litigation and debt combat, similarly, the conventional view is that all litigation revolves around the creditor, that only creditors can sue debtors, and that debtors are necessarily like the planets and sun circling the earth.

But Copernicus's Law of the Law holds otherwise: that in fact the world of litigation will revolve around him who strikes first and most aggressively. Debtors who break the bonds of medieval thinking and strike first, by filing their lawsuits against oppressive creditors, will soon discover that the world will revolve around them, and not vice versa.

Because of the Law of Conservation and Fungibility of Money, which holds that money can neither be created nor destroyed (it just changes hands) and that dollar bills are all interchangeable with one another, we can deduce that creditors will usually give up on their claims against aggressive debtors. It makes no economic sense for them to spend more money on legal fees than they stand to collect from the nonpaying debtors.

According to Copernicus's Law of the Law, litigation tactics are analogous to gravitational forces in the real world. By suing a creditor, the debtor will *ipso facto* generate very strong "gravitational" forces that will tend to bring the creditor to his knees (quite literally). The aggressive debtor can control the pace and extent of the litigation, use his tools to drain the creditor of money through a protracted and expensive war of attrition, and thereby bring him down.

It was none other than Aristotle who developed the "Theory of Natural Law," which held that in order to be successful in human relations, one must "emulate Nature" by copying the behavior of physical objects in one's personal behavior. That is why these physical laws, such as those discovered by

Copernicus (and, as we shall see, Newton and Einstein), are directly applicable to the debtor-creditor conflict.

So the debtor's goal is to use these applied physical laws to force a creditor to forgive or drastically reduce the debt owed him. But why would any creditor, the question may fairly be asked, deign to "forgive" a debtor's debt to which he is "lawfully" entitled?

But stop and think for a minute: Why should a creditor be entitled to win interest without having to work for it? Is this really fair?

Wise economists throughout the ages have often distinguished between "productive capital" and "unproductive capital." The former, consisting of things and services of value produced by a society, has been contrasted with the latter, a "paper game"—more recently a computerized cyberspace game—in which exorbitant rates of interest have come to replace productive capital as an income-generating activity. Few pause to think about it in these terms, but it is so.

CREDIT CARDS: THE USURY TOOLS OF THE MODERN AGE

Biblical pronouncements aside, one may well pause to wonder darkly about a system that thrives on usury, and in this system the credit card industry is the most usurious of all.

Corporate debt typically is charged an interest rate below 5 percent, and while the prime rate in recent decades has been well below 10 percent, the interest charged by banks and other credit companies on credit cards and other consumer debt has skyrocketed and hovered at about 20 percent or more.

Why should individuals be oppressed with an interest rate more than four times that applied to corporate debtors? Isn't there something inherently unfair about this two-faced scheme of lending money?

What is so inherently untrustworthy or risky about a consumer's prospects of debt repayment that justifies these exorbitant (and legal) interest rates?

Economists have calculated that to repay a credit card debt of $10,000, it will take an average American family forty years, because of the massive interest rates imposed. And the total amount this family must ultimately pay on the initial $10,000 debt is about $40,000.

But what entitles a moneylender to charge such a 400-percent "markup" for doing nothing productive with his money? Joe Debtor has no answer: He barely realizes that religiously making minimal monthly payments will get him nowhere, and that as much as 96 percent of such payments (in the early months of the loan) will go to paying off interest alone. Hence, once you become a debtor, for all practical purposes, you become an indentured serf for life—indentured to your faceless creditor.

Why, it may be fairly asked, should consumers have to pay out this usury and trap themselves in the bonds of debt for forty years?

It has been observed that if all debtors suddenly stopped paying on their credit cards, the banking-credit system would collapse overnight. As of mid-2002, the total amount of consumer credit card debt out there exceeded $400 billion. That is an astounding figure. What is even more astounding is that when one considers that at interest rates of as much as 22 percent (or even more) for consumer debt and credit card debt, that figure represents hundreds of millions in income to the banks of this country every year.

This is a situation analogous to that of scarce workers striking, or of motorists all exceeding the speed limit. The law simply cannot be enforced if everyone, a majority (or even a sizable minority), refuses to play ball under this extremely unfair system.

THE DIRECT ROUTE TO DEBT ERADICATION

What is to be done? What can be done?

Fortunately for the strapped consumer, there is another iron law of economics out there: a mathematical, economic law as inexorable in its logic as the vile system that keeps consumers yoked to the millstone. It is called the "Law of Fungibility of Money." This law holds that any particular batch of money is always interchangeable, which means that there is no difference between dollar "A" and dollar "B," since one can be freely substituted for the other. Hence, it makes no difference to a creditor where his money comes from or to where it goes. All that matters is the "bottom line."

At Harvard Business School, MBA students are taught that the only thing that counts in life is "the bottom line." That is, at the end of the day, all the creditor cares about is the net gain or loss of fungible dollars he has made.

Looking at the credit dilemma as a one-way street is like looking at a deep well from the bottom. Yes, the creditor has many mighty tools at his disposal; whips with which to lash the debtor and force him to pony up the cash; armies of lawyers; threats of reporting to the dreaded beast of collection; and damage to the consumer's credit report card through credit reporting agencies. Yes, these tools exist, but at a price, for lawyers do not come free, and neither do other tools and tradesmen of the debt collection industry.

It stands to reason that if a creditor is faced with the dire reality of having to spend more money on lawyer fees and related litigation costs to collect from a debtor, the rational creditor will bail out of such a game by settling for whatever he can get. A debtor with a credit card bill, loan, or other obligation of, let us say, $10,000, who can convince the creditor that he will be facing legal bills and attorney's fees of $10,000 has a lot of power in pursuing a negotiation with that creditor. It only stands to reason. The creditor is in the business of making money, and faced with the prospect of losing money, he will be searching for an escape.

An aware citizenry of debtors, armed with this valuable secret knowledge, can thus thwart the bullying tactics of even the most vile and ruthless creditor or collection agency.

Thus, the Law of Litigation Debt Eradication applies with its inexorable and ineluctable logic. It is a law as old as the ages, yet strangely enough, less than 5 percent of all debtors know about this law.

What is so sacred about this law of debt and collections? Nothing. Most people tend to view reality as a fixed system of laws, players, and rules that favor the banks. But not all rules favor the banks and creditors, and no rule is absolutely "fixed" in any sense. When the system is viewed from the outside, there is another set of rules that favors the debtor. Most debtors cannot fathom the revolutionary idea that every pro-creditor law or rule is just an arbitrary and negotiable obstacle on the road of life, an obstacle that can and should be challenged.

What is so sacred about a creditor's imposing usurious interest rates on debtors who cannot afford to pay? Nothing.

What is so sacred about one's credit history? Nothing.

Once a debtor arms himself with the mighty armor of Litigation Debt Eradication, he is armed as David was against Goliath. Why did David win with a slingshot? Because Goliath did not understand that even the smallest mouse can roar loudly enough to be heard, provided that the inexorable law of net averages is followed.

If the average debtor can hire a lawyer—or represent himself—in court against the creditors and could sue the creditor for torts and wrongs of all sorts, the average creditor will give up on the debt (or negotiate it down to a mere fraction of its value rather than spend more money on lawyers and court costs).

This is the key kernel of knowledge, which is rarely followed in our society, but which possesses the immense revolutionary power to transform millions of debtors overnight and empower them into an army capable of storming the ramparts of even the most resolute and ruthless creditor out there.

The average civil lawsuit in this country takes about fifteen months to come to trial. During those fifteen months, an empowered debtor can wreak such havoc against creditors that the debt-credit system can be turned upside down, on its head, inside out. This will enable the debtor to get out of debt, free and easy.

DEBT ERADICATION: THE AGGRESSIVE APPROACH

How can it be done?

Easily. First, debtors must become psychologically empowered to confront their creditors with a militant, aggressive, and self-confident attitude that brooks no resistance. Creditors are not used to real resistance. The letters they usually get are plaintive and caviling letters. A letter that promises countermeasures has an effect. We are not talking about bluffing, posturing letters. In the poker game of debt, a player who relies on the bluff will soon be discovered.

Second, empowered debtors must either hire a good debt lawyer or educate themselves in the most minimal lessons of litigation, which are taught in this book. The infamous legal letterhead works wonders. All things being equal, the letter on legal stationery will always go further than the letter without it. The mere fact of having representation raises the stakes for the credit company, and it conveys your seriousness. The first thing that legal stationery means is that you feel strongly enough to send your money to an attorney instead of to Joe Creditor.

Third, debtors must sue their creditors, either by striking

first as plaintiffs, or by striking second and counterattacking by filing cross-complaints (called countersuits or counterclaims in some states) against their creditors after being sued by the latter. In an existential sense, to file a lawsuit or countersuit is to cross a major legal and emotional barrier, a figurative Rubicon, in the credit wars. The creditor knows it and you know it.

Those three factors together—not only *acting* confident but *feeling* confident, hiring a lawyer, and filing suit—add up to dollar signs. The important factor is that those are dollar signs that are outgoing instead of incoming. And that impresses the creditors most of all. It is a numbers game to them and it has to become a numbers game to the debtor who wants to be empowered in the credit wars.

There is always a *casus belli* to entitle a debtor to sue a creditor, such as the exorbitant usurious interest rates charged, "late fees" charged arbitrarily even if the debtor has sent a payment on time, and a plethora of other arrows in the quiver.

The idea of a debtor suing a creditor is absolutely revolutionary. This is the "Spartacus Slave Revolt" of our time. After all, it's supposed to work the other way around. Creditors are supposed to be the good guys suing the bad guys—deadbeat debtors. So how can such deadbeat debtors possibly muster the absolute gall to sue their creditors? What effrontery, you say! What chutzpah!

To all of the above, we plead guilty. Yes, it takes nerve, chutzpah, and effrontery to strike out at one's oppressor, but thanks to our "open" court system, anyone in this country (noncitizens and citizens alike) has a legal right to sue anyone else for anything at any time. The limits are only those self-imposed, such as fear, trepidation, guilt, ignorance, timidity, dissonance, and other chimera of the mind. Some of that trepidation is good. It takes careful planning to beat the creditors at their own game, and such a course should not be undertaken lightly. But most of that fear is created by creditors solely for the purpose of brainwashing and conditioning their debtor slaves to pay up or else. With knowledge and careful planning it is possible to break the chains of debt and be empowered to fight back.

Why would anyone in his right mind take on a major bank in a lawsuit? How can David beat Goliath, or even last a round in the ring?

It takes knowledge and persistence, but it can be done. The answer lies in the inexorable logic of economics, and the law of fungibility of money.

And what of the extension of the physical laws to debt management litigation? The physical "laws" describe immutable facts about the real physical world. Since human beings are a part of this world, it follows that these inexorable laws should apply to describe their behavior. How can one go wrong when he or she acts according to the physical laws?

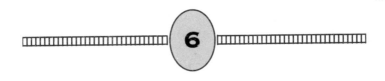

Litigation: Debt
Eradication in Practice

WE KNOW THAT the number of lawsuits filed every year has dramatically increased over the past twenty years. Yet surprisingly few involve a debtor suing a creditor for such things as breach of contract, fraud, breach of warranty, debt collection harassment, and the like.

Psychological studies show how debtors generally adopt the mentality of "defendants" and "criminals," so they cannot imagine themselves as plaintiffs vis-à-vis their creditors. After all, how can one who *owes money*—actual money—sue the entity to which money is owed? Above all, how can a person who is already deeply in debt afford to hire a lawyer to sue his creditors? How can a debtor unschooled in the law represent himself, for is it not true that "He who represents himself has a fool for a client"?

Creditors generally rely on this "guilt-laden" mentality in their prey, to roll over them by harassment, threats, and lawsuits. Because they know that debtors are generally deeply embarrassed about owing money, being unable to pay their bills, and are disabled by insecurity and guilt, creditors believe that they will get a free ride.

THROWING OFF THE MANTLE OF GUILT

But it really doesn't have to be this way. Obtaining "debtor consciousness" is necessary in order that the debtor may feel qualified and entitled to sue the creditor.

The first step for the debtor is to realize that suing somebody is a very unpredictable and arbitrary act of *gambling*. The court system is extremely irrational and unpredictable, like a gambling casino or stock market. *There is nothing certain in the law*. As any honest and experienced litigator will tell you, the outcome of a trial can never be predicted with certainty, even under seemingly irrefutable facts. A courtroom is nothing more than a sophisticated gambling casino. A judge and jury are no more than glorified one-arm bandits, human slot machines that take your money, invite you to pull their levers, and tempt you with the glittering promise of a jackpot.

Is it fool's gold at the end of a rainbow? Ask any gambler in Reno or Vegas, and you will receive a very interesting answer.

NEWTON'S FIRST LAW: RISK FOR THE CREDITOR

This brings us to what I call "Newton's First Law of the Law," to wit, that, "For every trial verdict, there is an equal and opposite verdict." What this means is that one can never be sure how a trial will turn out, and therefore it is this inherent uncertainty that makes creditors cringe at the very thought that their debtors will sue them (or countersue them).

Why is Newton's First Law true? For several reasons. First, because the written law is itself hopelessly ambiguous in the way it is written and interpreted by various and sundry courts. This is the main reason why lawyers argue ad infinitum about who is right and wrong: We don't know, because the law is so ambiguous. *We just don't know what it means.* The written law appears to be clear, but in applicability it is like a Rorschach test: Different people see different things in it. Legislators, both federal and state ones, typically inject a strong dose of ambiguity into all of the statutes they enact, as a way of reaching a compromise so that they can get enough votes to enact the law. Ambiguity is attractive because it can lead legislators on both side of the aisle to read whatever they want into the statute, and to gamble that future judges interpreting the statutes will rule in their favor. Hence, Rorschach is the true Lord of the Laws.

Next, Newton's First Law is true because juries are made up of laypersons who are generally unschooled in the law and who usually react mainly on the basis of emotion rather than reason. These twelve laypersons often practice what lawyers and judges call "jury nullification," meaning that they seem to disregard the "evidence" presented at trial and find in favor of the party whom they like the best. Juries generally feel *simpatico* with one party, based on the histrionics and inherent uncertainties of the plaintiff and defendant and their counsel. What this means is that, for example, a sympathetic debtor—such as an impecunious widow—will appear far more worthy of the jurors' empathy than will a ruthless corporate creditor.

And last—but not least—Newton's First Law is true because there are so many distinct and different courts in each state and the country that statistical averages will come into play and will necessarily result in conflicting opinions, both as to trial verdict and judicial interpretations of the law. This is analogous to flipping a coin thousands of times: The number of heads is likely to be very similar to the number of tails.

In some cases, trials are conducted by a judge, not a jury. These are called "court trials." But the underlying dynamics are the same: The judge is just a man in a black robe. Two judges will interpret a Rorschach blot in radically different ways; in the same way, they will interpret differently the law and evidence in your case. Short of bribery and favoritism, a judge is just another "thirteenth juror."

With judge or jury as trier of fact, you can never be sure of the outcome. This is what makes creditors shake in their boots: Short of bribery or extortion, they can *never* be sure that they will prevail in court.

NEWTON'S SECOND LAW: UNIVERSAL JUSTIFICATION

This "flipping of the coin" phenomenon leads us to "Newton's Second Law of the Law," to wit: For each and every published court opinion rendered by a judge, there is an equal and opposite opinion on the very same issue that can be found somewhere in the law books. In legal research and brief writing, the trench warfare of the litigation process, one can virtually always find contradictory court opinions on the very same issue, which means that the outcome of a legal case is always uncertain. In the "law and motion" practice before trials—where lawyers churn out thousands of pages of meaningless and contradictory legalese mumbo-jumbo and argue in pro forma hearings before a bored and listless judge—plaintiffs and defendants typically spar with each other by filing briefs that cite cases reported in state and federal "court reporters," available in any law library. While each lawyer presents his cited cases as gospel truth, in practice he is presenting but one case out of many, and it is the duty of the opposing counsel or party to counter Case Precedent A with Case Precedent B. Because this is the prevailing gamesmanship in any case, law students in their "moot court" classes in law school are taught to always argue both sides of every case that they study.

What this means for our purposes is that any rational creditor (and his armies of expensive attorneys) who is faced with a lawsuit by a debtor against him has to factor in this uncertainty, in addition to the certainty of having to pay out massive legal fees to defend himself against the debtor's suit and to bring suit against the debtor.

NEWTON'S THIRD LAW: WHAT GOES UP MUST COME DOWN

This leads us to Newton's Third Law of the Law, to wit: Whatever goes up in court, must come down. As with the inexorable law of gravity, so it is inside the courtroom. Newton's Third Law of the Law simply means that if a creditor tries to "defend" himself against the debtor-plaintiff in a lawsuit or countersuit where the creditor is put on the defensive, he must pay out a massive amount of money to lawyers and other parasites of the legal system. This includes massive "administrative" costs (such as discovery costs, process servers, subpoenas, humongous fees for the hiring of expert witnesses, jury consultants, etc.). Yes, the creditor may toss his ball of "evidence" up in the air, but that ball will come crashing back down on his head because of the "weight" of his costs. It may inflict greater damage on the creditor than he could possibly gain by "winning" his case in court against the debtor. Even if he "wins," the creditor always "loses."

Because of Newton's Third Law of the Law, any rational creditor must realize that the act of suing the debtor (throwing the ball into the air) will be pointless if he has to pay out more money in litigation costs than he can possibly hope to recover from the debtor.

If the debtor can persuasively convince the creditor that he is in the game for the long haul, and that he will fight hard and long, the creditor will have to "reassess" his strategy and inevitably make a deal for pennies on the dollar, or give up altogether.

After twenty-seven years of law practice, this author has never ceased to be amazed by how easily even the most truculent-looking creditors have caved in when faced with a cross-complaint or lawsuit by a debtor against them. Great universities suing debtors on student loans, huge banks suing debtors for default on mortgages or credit cards, and yes, even the mighty IRS itself suing debtor taxpayers in tax court, have caved in and cried the magic words for Uncle:

"It's just not worth it!"

Those are the magic words the debtor wants to hear, for they mean that the creditor will give up, make a deal for cents on the dollar debt, remove deleterious and libelous information on the debtor's credit reports, and/or quit his debt collection campaign altogether.

"It's just not worth it!"

But what if the debtor loses his trial, you say? Won't an unsuccessful debtor be penalized for bringing a "frivolous" lawsuit or counterclaim against a "legitimate" creditor?

Fortunately, the answer is a resounding, "No!" In the United States, courts do not have a rule requiring the loser to pay the attorney fees of the winner, in any suit or counter suit, except in rare instances where a contract mandates the paying of attorney fees by the loser. While other countries, such as England, do have such laws in general, we do not.

At worst, an unsuccessful debtor-litigator would be hit with a "bill of costs" of perhaps up to a few thousand dollars for such things as deposition costs and postage and copying. But even this is generally negotiable and the losing debtor can almost always easily obtain a waiver of the bill of costs, if he waives his right to appeal an unfavorable outcome, as a quid pro quo. Generally, winning creditors will be more than happy to waive their bill of costs because they know that it will cost them far more money for legal fees and costs to oppose a lengthy appeal than they could possibly hope to collect from the losing debtor.

Newton's Laws again kick in, and save the debtor even if he loses. Because of the availability of automatic appeals, the debtor has a safety net at all times during the litigation. Losing parties all have an automatic right to appeal an unfavorable outcome to the first tier of appeal courts in their state, and in the federal system. Appeals generally take an average of eighteen months, and the clever debtor-litigator can delay the process by repeatedly requesting continuances for filing of briefs, and can easily drag the time out to two years or beyond. If he loses in the first appeal court, he may try to appeal further up the chain to the state supreme court, and if that fails, to the U.S. Supreme Court.

In law, unlike baseball and football and life itself, there *is* always "life after losing." At least for a while . . . a *very expensive while* for the creditors.

The appeal courts and supreme courts also follow Newton's First and Second and Third Laws, so that there is always an inherent uncertainty facing even the most successful creditor-litigator on appeal.

But wait a moment! Whoa! Hold the horses! All this may be fine and dandy in theory, you say, but what about in fact? While *a priori* reasoning may make sense, what about *a posteriori*, "blood and guts," actual workings of the law in fact? Can a debtor "make up" claims and counterclaims against a "legitimate" creditor? Is it ethical to "make up" such claims when they may not exist in fact, or may have been concocted in the debtor's mind?

Ah, yes, here comes the dreaded "Beast of Ethics," the *bête noire* of even the most hardy and hearty debtor.

What about ethics? Indeed.

EINSTEIN'S LAW:
RELATIVITY SERVES THE DEBTOR AS WELL

To answer this question, we graduate from Newton's Laws of the Law to Einstein's Law of the Law. Just as Einstein's laws of physics supplemented Newton's, so it is in the law.

Albert Einstein, the genius physicist, is remembered mainly for his "Theory of Relativity," which held that there is no "absolute" frame of reference in the physical world, and that therefore one's observations depend on his frame of reference. As an example Einstein gave, a passenger on Train A sitting still in the train station sees Train B coming at him and measures its velocity as 60 mph. But another passenger on Train C, which is racing toward Train B at a speed of 80 mph, sees Train B's velocity to be 140 mph (a combination of 60 and 80 mph).

Who is "right"? Passenger A or C?

Einstein would say, "Neither and both, because motion is relative to one's frame of reference." In Einsteinian theory, there is no absolute frame of reference in the real world. Extrapolated to our area of the law, Einstein's Law of Legal Relativity similarly holds that what one perceives as "truth" is relative to one's frame of reference, in every sense, and that there is no absolute frame of reference for ethical standards.

In the Bible, there is an extremely important, haunting question asked, which has echoed for twenty centuries. It was put to Jesus by Pontius Pilate: *Quod est Veritas?* ("What is truth?") Significantly, Jesus did not answer the question. He left it to us to decide.

Neither can we answer the question, absolutely. Neither can a jury or a judge.

Einstein's Law of Legal Relativity thus maintains that there is no absolute rendition of evidence that can be absolutely declared correct or incorrect. Two different juries or judges may well perceive different versions of reality, when examining exactly the same set of facts presented.

This does not mean that one should lie or make up allegations out of whole cloth, for that would be perjury per se. What it does mean is simply that if the debtor can come up with any conceivable circumstances and nuances that are important in his case, he should marshal all his facts and present them, in the form of a lawsuit or countersuit against his creditors.

To give but one quick and easy example of how Einstein's Law of Legal Relativity can be put into effect in a lawsuit or countersuit by a debtor, consider the following scenario: Karen is a divorced mother of two and is struggling to make ends meet. A fast-talking salesman comes to her door and persuades her to buy a $3,000 dishwasher by charging it on her Visa card. He makes several representations to her, as to what the product can do, its quality, etc., and she believes him. After the machine is delivered, it fails to meet up to the expectations "promised" by the salesman. She writes to Visa and to the vendor and informs them of the chicanery, but they all ignore her, refuse to take the machine back, and remind her, "A contract is a contract! . . . You signed the contract." End of story.

What can Karen do? She can either give up, or withhold monthly payments and wait to get sued by the Visa card issuer or collection agency, and see her credit rating plummet. Or she can sue the vendor and the Visa company and its collection agents for fraud, breach of warranty, breach of contract, infliction of emotional distress, breach of covenant of good faith and fair dealing, violation of state and federal consumer protection acts, violation of fair debt collection practices acts, and any number of other possibilities.

If Karen strikes out at her oppressors by filing suit (the sooner the better, before her credit is damaged too severely as more time goes by), she will thereby invoke Newton's Three Laws and take the creditor and vendor, to the mat. Before she knows it, the credit card company, vendor, and collectors will be countersuing each other for indemnification and so on. She will have kicked up a mighty storm of chaos based on an inherently uncertain and unpredictable legal system, in which the only laws that apply are Newton's and Einstein's.

PENNIES ON THE DOLLAR: SOME PRACTICAL EXAMPLES

Chances are, the creditor and vendor will take back the machine or settle their claim against her for pennies on the dollar, if sued.

A particular case will serve to represent a common scenario. A woman—let's call her Helen—had chalked up debt of $30,000 on a MasterCard through a major West Coast bank. The bank imposed the usual "late fees" arbitrarily, claiming the woman had sent in payment a day or more late, and had turned an original debt of $16,000 into nearly twice that amount in a few short years.

Eventually, Helen—a single mom with three youngsters— lost her job and developed breast cancer, finding it impossible to continue making payments. She found that unless she adopted a policy of selective credit payment and paid only her mortgage, she and her kids would be turned out into the streets.

What to do? Like most people, the woman in question felt a "moral" obligation to pay her credit card debts on time.

After she had gone through much soul searching and guilt cleansing, a competent attorney (this author) convinced Helen to sue the bank for credit fraud and credit defamation, as well as for breach of contract, fraud, and a plethora of other causes of action.

At first, the bank responded by ignoring her completely. The relentless threatening letters pelted her and she reeled from the onslaught. The faceless collection agency was soon replaced by the faceless lawyers who threatened to sue her until her children were at retirement age, or until she was reduced to poverty, whichever came first.

Once the process server hand-filed the woman's suit on the bank, a remarkable transformation occurred. After a short interlude, in which the phone calls and letters continued, they soon came to a screeching halt. Changing her phone number and post office box address had not stopped the collection monster or the continuing threats of legal harassment, but suing almost instantly did the trick.

Helen's attorney immediately bombarded the bank with 500 interrogatories; 372 requests for production of documents, and notices for 56 depositions of its top officials and officers, including the CEO; 276 vice presidents; and 43 collection officers. The bank, faced with this massive onslaught, found itself reeling.

This wasn't supposed to happen in the faceless world of credit collection! Debtors were supposed to be on the receiving end of lawsuits, not on the attacking end. The bank simply did not know what to do. The feckless collection agency to which it had sold the woman's debts was equally dumbfounded. For starters, both the bank and the collection agency had to hire lawyers at $300 per hour (plus costs), with an initial retainer down payment of $10,000 each.

The bank and the collection agency operating jointly (since they were bound by a contractual relationship) had to face the prospect of losing $20,000 right off the bat. The bank now began to wonder what was to be gained by hounding a woman for $30,000 in debt.

Though the bank never admitted this, Helen and her lawyer were fortunate enough to overhear the bank's negotiators (a bank officer and several of their attorneys) in a voice mail message when someone had unwittingly failed to hang up while they discussed the debtor's case.

"Do you think she will go for that?" the bank officer asked.

The attorneys in answer advised that the bank would be wise to take whatever counteroffer Helen's attorney might recommend. They agreed that costs would quickly put them into buckets of red ink even if there were a shadowy prospect of full payment down the road.

The reality is that any settlement is going to be a fraction of the total amount, while the red ink is mounting with each tick of the clock. In this instance, delay is on the side of the debtor who is suing, because the bills for litigation are coming in with a regularity that the bank soon finds alarming.

It is a fact well concealed by the legal system, the bar associations, and the entrenched monied interests in the law, but it is nonetheless true, that there is no certainty in the law. If a case gets to trial, there is no way to predict how a jury will vote, as any experienced trial barrister will readily admit. (Avoid like the plague any attorney who will not admit this. If an attorney puts up a false front of "certainty" and claims that the outcome of your case is as certain as the sun's rising tomorrow from the east, step out into the hallway to get a drink of water and run like hell.)

In general, as any seasoned trial lawyer will tell you, juries are a wholly irrational entity, an institution that reacts mainly on the basis of emotion and chance, not logic. Our jury system is much celebrated by screenwriters and the editorial boards of newspapers primarily because these writers don't understand the system in action, and prefer to glorify an abstract fairy tale. In reality, juries are in the box to be manipulated and dazzled primarily with emotion rather than reason, and the big expensive corporate lawyers with money to burn will hire shadow juries and focus groups to test market their jury appeals. The corporations will pay that kind of money to protect themselves from million-dollar liability verdicts, but they are not going to spend it on debtor suits disputing $30,000 or less.

Helen won at the end of the day. The bank settled for

$1,000 as "payment in full" for the $30,000 debt, and counted itself lucky to get even that. Helen also got the bank to agree to write to the infamous myrmidons of the credit world, the credit reporting bureaus, to remove all allegations of "delinquency and default" from her record.

Helen had to pay a legal fee. But she got a lot for her money. She got peace of mind and a sense of empowerment that she will carry with her for the rest of her life. Most of all, she got the tools to protect herself if she ever found herself in this circumstance again.

Was this ethical? Was the mass attack of thousands of interrogatories, and calculated delaying of the case, ethical?

"In law and war, all is fair," is the response.

When approaching combat against morally dubious corporations, whose representative paragons are the likes of Enron and WorldCom, it is necessary for the debtor to arm himself or herself with the moral armor of God and go forward into battle. Corporate America, with its routine "creative accounting" chicanery and outright fraud and theft of assets by its unscrupulous CEOs and other managers, has absolutely forfeited any moral right it may once have enjoyed to force debtors to pony up money to "pay their bills." What right has a morally bankrupt company or bank got to remind the rest of us to pay our bills? What ethical basis does an Enron or a WorldCom (or their millions of analogues scattered throughout the wasteland of corporate America) have to force the little guy to finance the sybaritic lifestyle of its "rich and famous" executives? These same corporate executives who routinely milk the company by rewarding themselves for their incompetence and greed by sucking up millions of dollars in salaries, perks, stock options, and golden parachutes.

To choose a more dramatic, "manifold Helen" example, a few years ago, "Visa International" and some other credit card issuers began arbitrarily imposing a legally dubious "currency conversion fee" on Visa cardholders whenever they purchased something overseas in a foreign currency. The millions of credit card holders had never been asked for their consent before such a conversion fee was imposed, yet the banks arrogantly imposed it sneakily.

A group of credit card users decided to file a huge class action against the banks, on behalf of all the millions of similarly situated card holders. In 2003, a California court found in favor of the card holders, and imposed billions of dollars of penalties on the bad guys, finding that the imposition of the conversion fees constituted fraud and breach of contract.

Yet credit card issuers impose such illegal and arbitrary fees every day, without the consent of their customers. They *can and should be sued relentlessly for this illegal chicanery.* Even the mere threat of such a monster class action suit can deter the bad guys and force them to come to the conference table.

Every debtor possesses the ability to launch such a guerrilla war class action suit, any time, anywhere.

Having begun this chapter with analogies to physical laws, let us close it out with a law from military science. I call this Clausewitz's Law of the Law, and it goes like this: Litigation is the Continuation of Business by Other Means!

The 11th Commandment: "Debtor, Protect Thy Assets"

THE ULTIMATE GOAL in the "chase the debtor" game is for the creditor to seize the assets of the debtor. After all, it would make no sense to spend a fortune on legal fees chasing someone who has no assets, or who appears to have little or no assets.

Generally, creditors go through the ritual of courtroom brawling in order to obtain that coveted Final Judgment, a document that enables them to seize the debtor's house, car, antique collection, salary, etc.

But what if it appeared that the debtor has no collectable assets? Would a rational creditor go after him then?

Each year, banks and other creditors "write off" literally billions of dollars of "uncollectable debt." They then lower their own taxable income by that amount, and this often has rich rewards by lowering their tax rates. In an era where tax evasion is the natural language of most Americans, the creditors have much to gain by manipulating this rule.

Thus, Joe Debtor need not feel guilty about stiffing a creditor.

Chances are that the bad guy will write off the debt and reap a huge tax reward anyway. And he does not have to spend any money paying pettifoggers to plough through the courtroom.

Indeed, one of the major reasons why creditors are so eager to write off bad debts, or at least to write off a large majority of the total amount due, is this "second life" of tax reduction.

We all hate taxes. Ronald Reagan and his progeny of conservative politicos have made it a national religion to hate taxes, to lower taxes, to cut taxes. Well, the Reaganites' corporate sponsors—largely card-carrying members of the "creditor" juggernaut—would love to cut their taxes by writing off a huge portion of their debts as uncollectable.

Creditors make these decisions every day, "to sue or not to sue, to write off or not to write off a bad debt." They play this game out of sight and out of sound, but I can assure you that they do play it. And one of the criteria they look at is whether the debtor has any collectable assets.

At this point, we must turn quasi-religious and instill in the debtor's mind an idea that should be called "The 11th Commandment." And that is, "PROTECT THY ASSETS."

Unless the debtor has an effective strategy to protect his assets from hungry creditors, he is in trouble, because the wolves will salivate at the prospect of seizing his house, car, and other assests. Just as countries protect their borders, people, and children by building large armaments, walls, and moats, so too the debtor must protect his assets by building impenetrable defenses around them.

Sun Tzu, the ancient Chinese warrior and philosopher who wrote *The Art of War*, once said that "Every battle is won before it has even begun."

In Sun Tzu's lingo, a debtor can expect to "win" his battle against a hungry creditor if he manages to convince the creditor that he has little or no assets that can be seized, even in the event of a victory in court.

If the debtor can do this, he can paralyze his foe right at the outset and deter the latter from even bothering to sue for the debt. Like some insects, such as the stink bugs, that emit vile, poisonous, malodorous whiffs that paralyze their foe and ward him off, debtors too can convince creditors to turn the other cheek and go away peacefully, simply by convincing the latter that they have no assets.

In legal lingo, these types of debtors are called "judgment-proof," or "JP." The instant a creditor is convinced that a debtor is JP, he will write off the bad debt and claim relief from Uncle Sam through the tax code.

The Practical Alternatives of Asset Protection

There are a number of practical things that every person with assets can do to protect himself from the predation of hungry judgment seekers. First, it cannot be underestimated how much keeping a low profile can help. The more homes that a person owns in the rich part of town, with garages full of premium automobiles, are all going to trigger the wrong kinds of automatic reactions in the creditor or potential creditor. A creditor forms his first impression from your address. A modest office in a modest building or even a post office box will work so much better than 1000 Mansion Row.

Second, a modest investment in basic liability and home-owner's insurance might be advisable in certain circumstances. The insurance game is fraught with peril and is outside of the scope of this book, and certainly insurance companies can rip you off and be just as risky as any other gambit. However, insurance can cover some of the more realistic and basic risks to your assets.

Third, begin to structure your affairs so that you become an unattractive target for the ambitious creditor or his lawyer who might be tempted to dip his hands into your pockets because he has the impression that they might be deep. One of the first gambits that is allowed in some states and not others is called homestead protection. It may allow you to place an umbrella over your house, retirement account, annuities, and other accounts. After that, you might consider the advantages to setting up a partnership to protect your personal assets. There are vehicles called Family Limited Partnerships that accept the transfer of your assets and can then be used for estate planning and for other sorts of financial planning. It is just one of the ways that may make it difficult for judgment seekers to find out what your true assets are and then even harder to get their hands on them.

Fourth, place your assets in creditor-hostile entities where it is not just difficult but actually impossible for a judgment seeker or his lawyer to get his hands on those assets. The main possibilities are domestic corporations and limited liability companies where assets can be under your control but not subject to a judgment against you personally. The more esoteric possibilities include the foreign corporation. This may sound obscure and difficult, but it is done all of the time and has been successful for an enormous number of people. It may conjure up visions of living on remote Caribbean islands with drug kingpins and the Shah of Iran, but it is perfectly legal, and in some circumstances practical.

A subset of the above asset protection hostile entity is the foreign or domestic trust. There are an enormous number of various kinds of trusts and each of them has its own tax advantages. In fact, trusts are usually thought of as tax avoidance devices and that too is outside of the scope of this book. But they are also effective in taking assets outside of the scope of a judgment seeker. They should be considered carefully for their unique advantages.

HIDING ASSETS LEGITIMATELY
AND LEGALLY

Now, how can one legitimately hide assets from creditors? And what does "legitimate" mean in this context? Is this moral, equitable, legal, or sane? What are the risks involved?

Clearly, the debtor seeking to enforce the 11th Commandment must follow Jesus' advice to be "wise as serpents and clever as foxes," for he goes out into a world of "wolves."

Now the clever fox specializes in the strategy of Indirect Approach, because that is the strategy least likely to attract the attention and venom of the creditor snakes. He avoids "fraudulent conveyances and transfers" to a close relative or friend, and he does not take on the creditor directly by transferring an asset right under the creditor's nose. To do so would be to invite massive retaliation on the creditor's own turf, and that is what we seek to prevent at all costs.

The Indirect Approach can be applied in credit wars just as it can in real wars. What it means, in military science, is that the debtor will keep the creditor guessing as to where his assets are, and whether they exist at all, until the bad guy goes away and writes off the debt.

Timing is critical in the Indirect Approach. If you are a debtor and you see an imminent cash flow problem on the horizon, you should consider putting the 11th Commandment into effect ASAP, and before any legal action is initiated against you.

If you have been sued and the process server is beating down your door to serve you with summons and a complaint, it is generally too late to legally protect your assets by transferring them to a relative or friend. A transfer like this will generally be struck down by the courts as fraudulent.

But if you transfer your assets to a trusted *compadre* before the creditors start banging on your door, you can generally get away with this as a safe and legal transaction.

Rich people know this and do it all the time, though often for reasons other than debt avoidance. They transfer assets to their children, spouses, grandchildren, siblings, and trusted associates, generally to evade taxes, both in vivo and post vivo.

A rather notorious sybarite in the San Francisco Bay Area, "Mad Max," played this game with aplomb and managed to avoid taxes like the proverbial will-o'-the-wisp. He transferred his million-dollar house to his wife, his yacht to his daughter, and his stocks and bonds to his nieces and nephews. The result was that he was "judgment proof," because the transfers had taken place before the process server arrived at his doorstep.

The man lived like a king, all the while claiming he had "no assets."

In a literal sense, he was right.

When a creditor sees this, he turns the other way. Indeed, Mad Max managed to deflect lawsuits from business rivals and victims and others, by posing as a "No Asset" player. He did this for thirty years, paid no taxes, and lived the life of a jet setter.

Few debtors think of emulating the lifestyles of the rich and famous in this way. Debtors are generally too "ashamed" and too embarrassed, groping about in their miasma of guilt and fear, to think about this.

Besides transferring their assets to trusted relatives and friends, debtors can also protect and shield their assets by transferring them to "offshore" banks and other repositories—again borrowing a technique routinely used by wealthy people to evade debts and taxes.

What is an "offshore" repository for assets? Who runs it? Is it safe? Is it legal?"

As with most things, the answer to this question is, "It depends."

Offshore asset havens are typically tiny islands literally situated "off the shore" (i.e., in the Caribbean Sea or elsewhere, such as the Cayman Islands, Bermuda, Barbados, and the like).

Wealthy Americans frequently hide their assets there in order to shield them from the IRS and from creditors.

What makes offshore havens attractive, as a magnet for assets, is that there are few "authorities" there to watch what is going on. Offshore banks, investment vehicles, and other entities act as money laundries, "washing" assets the debtor seeks to conceal from creditors at home, and hiding them with the wash.

The reliability of an offshore asset haven depends on who is running the show. Ringmasters range from legitimate bankers and financiers to outright pirates and con men.

Because offshore deposited assets cannot be traced very easily, they simply vanish into a black hole, and few creditors spend the time and resources to locate them. In addition, there are generally no income taxes and no luxury taxes in offshore banana republics. Thus, you will not be taxed on interest or profits there. Indeed, several huge American companies have recently taken advantage of this tax shelter game, and relocated their headquarters offshore to legally evade U.S. taxes. So much for the much vaunted "patriotism" of corporate America—your friendly creditors.

But what is good for the goose is certainly good for the gander.

Of course, it is illegal to "conceal" assets offshore from the IRS and to lie about possessing them under oath if you are sued in court by your creditors. These complications make this option for asset protection a very dicey affair.

Far better it is to fight your creditors in the court arena "inshore" than to seek shelter from dubious entities "offshore." But this is an issue for each debtor to decide, after searching his own conscience—and his own law books.

PART II

CREDITORS SUE DEBTORS: THE DEBTOR ON THE DEFENSE

MEDICAL BILL COLLECTIONS: THE "SPEEDY GONZALEZ" OF THE CREDIT MONSTERS

OF ALL THE CREDITOR PESTS out there, there are no creditors more aggressive and ravenous in collecting money than those involved in medical collections. Studies show that medical collections agencies, hospitals, doctors' offices, and the like are more likely to round up cash from cash-strapped debtors than any other form of collector.

Why is this?

Partly because Americans tend to respect doctors more than any other profession, partly because doctors wield an illusory power called "Your Money or Your Life!," and partly because doctors so dazzle us with their sophisticated technology.

As the cost of medical treatment has skyrocketed up to 20 percent higher annually, far higher than the rate of inflation, patients have continued to allow medical scam artists to pick their pockets clean with ease.

"YOUR MONEY OR YOUR LIFE!"

We live in a culture that wants to believe in the mirage of eternal youth, eternal life (here on earth), and eternal health. A plethora of movies and novels, in which dead people come back to earth in other guises, attest to this deep longing for eternal life on earth. People continue to believe in "near death" experiences from which they are miraculously rescued by the Eternal Doctor. Because people tend to see doctors as saviors, rather than as cold-hearted Shylocks, they tend to pony up their money to pay the doctor for "saving" their lives.

But it need not be so. It should not be so.

In reality, doctors are the Super Shylocks of our time. As the rate of medical incompetence and malpractice has risen, so too have medical bills. As HMOs, health plans, and medical merger-acquisition binges have turned Big Medicine into a structure as convoluted and impenetrable as the Palace Labyrinth of King Minos, the public has not shown the slightest signs of revolt. This blatantly corrupt and morally bankrupt billing system cares far more about the bottom line than it does about the flatline.

Why have medical bills escalated by over 20 percent each year?

One reason is the absurdly disproportionate rate of growth in medical costs, a phenomenon that we might term "medical inflation." Another reason is the absurdly arcane and anachronistic "patient pays" nature of the medical industry in the United States. Doctors and hospitals are the most likely collectors to take a debtor to "collections" and to sue the debtor. Because of the size of the sums involved there is a feeding frenzy that has developed in the collections industry, which attaches itself to hospitals and doctors and is devoted to squeezing every last shilling out of the hapless patient.

The reality of this industry is all too well represented by the old joke that a doctor will give his wealthy patient the diagnosis of a critical disease and then treat him until he is too poor to pay any more.

Medical billing chicanery is especially cruel because the consumer is never more vulnerable then when faced with the Grim Reaper in the guise of the inscrutable monolith of the medical establishment. When one of our loved ones is faced with a crisis where his or her life hangs in the balance, the first thing we tend to say to the doctor is: "Do anything you can. Cost is no object."

Doctors exploit this desperate state of mind and gouge people with the seldom-expressed but well-understood mantra, *Your Money or Your Life.*

At a time when every other civilized country in the world has the government paying all medical bills for all citizens, the United States is stuck back in the Wild West days, in which medical outlaws storm into town and force everyone to cough up their last buck to pay for medical care.

With a typical day in the hospital costing ten times more than the presidential suite at the most luxurious hotel in town, is it any wonder why the outlaws have scored so well? If the presidential suite at the Fairmont Hotel in San Francisco costs $10,000 per night, while a small room in St. Francis Hospital, a stone's throw down the street, costs $20,000 on average, can there be any doubt as to why the doctors are making out like bandits?

THE INSURANCE COMPANY AS GUARANTOR: THE GRAND ILLUSION

One of the main reasons why medical debtors do not see the precariousness of their position is that they tend to rely on "health insurance." No matter how high the charge of unnecessary and excessive high-tech "testing" recommended by the Man in the White Coat, Joe Patient is likely to say, "Okay" because of his belief that he is insured.

After all, when the Men in White ask for your "insurance card" before they even admit you through their hallowed gates, does this not mean you are taken care of?

As with most things in corporate America these days, the reality is something far different. Though insurance is supposed to pay for all medical treatment, insurance (medical and otherwise) is actually just a poor player in the carefully choreographed stage play of "Doctor Saves Patient." While health insurance pays a portion of the bill, the patient is typically left holding the bag for a huge amount, as a "deductible." Even more nefariously, insurance companies lately have been playing the "suck and sink" game, by plunging into bankruptcy after their executives have sucked all the money out of their coffers through lavish "bonuses and stock options" and the like. The number of insurance company bankruptcies has skyrocketed in the past five years, to the point where any trial lawyer will tell you that the consumer can no longer count on the insurance company to bail him out.

What most people don't understand is that insurance is no guarantee against "medical catastrophe": if your insurance carrier goes bankrupt (after playing the "Enron/WorldCom Game"), you will be left holding the bills, no matter how much cash you have ponied up in premiums over the years.

But whether with or *sans* insurance backup, every patient can expect to be hit hard—very hard—in the pocketbook by the Men in White. In the cold light of reason, as you try to balance your checkbook weeks or months later, you will understand too late how the doctors, the hospital, and indeed the entire medical establishment depends on our vulnerability and suspension of judgment to clean you out.

Yet, as with every other debtor-creditor conflict, there is a mighty arsenal of tools to fight back with. Paradoxically, medical creditors are among the easiest to combat in the ring of the courtroom.

Medical collectors are indeed the Speedy Gonzalezes of credit collection activity, but only because we let them assume this role.

COUNTERATTACK IN THE MEDICAL ARENA

Speedy Gonzalez was fast, but he was also puny and subject to immense counterattack.

Medical collectors are indeed the vultures of the collection war machine. Typically, when a person is injured or sick, he or she goes to the hospital and presents "proof of insurance." In the old days, the "triage nurse" was the person who made an initial diagnosis so that medical resources would be directed appropriately. Now the triage nurse is the person who checks your ability to pay. For those unfortunate enough to be uninsured or underinsured, the medical provider will either point toward the exit door (this is a practice known as "patient dumping") or will perform examination and treatment and follow that up with a massive medical bill.

Yet medical providers are subject to the easiest form of cross-complaint and credit dispute. The premise of all purchase contracts is that you got something for your money. The difficulty of proving that you got something for your money from the doctor or hospital may make the medical bill one of the most problematic purchase contracts in all the credit battlefield. This is because medical science is inexact at best. It is very difficult to prove what was the cause of an illness or injury, and it is even more difficult to prove whether the treatment proffered was effective in curing the malady.

Medical malpractice suits have been on the rise for the past twenty-five years, and most states now have statutes that limit the amount of damages a victim can collect against a doctor, hospital, or other healthcare provider. In California, this law is called "MICRA" and limits damages to $250,000. But $250,000 is more than enough to provide the debtor with an immensely powerful legal weapon, the malpractice suit.

Once a medical crisis is over, few of us are afraid of the arrogant individuals that we once laughingly referred to as MDs. We have all seen the statistics of studies that show one in six dosages given in a hospital is wrong in some respect. We have seen the medical recalls on the news and heard the horror stories of prescriptions written without checking the conflicts with other medications. In all too many instances the medical establishment does more harm that good.

The standard for malpractice in the courtroom is whether the medical provider "fell below the standard of care for a health professional in that area of practice." What is meant by the term "area" is both geographical area (typically, within a 100-mile radius of the city where the treatment was rendered), as well as the area of medical specialty (e.g., emergency room operations, plastic surgery, cardiology, oncology, neurology, etc.).

The problem with this "standard of care" shibboleth is that it is so vague as to be virtually meaningless in most cases. If you have shoulder pain and the doctor punctures your lung with a needle, and you fall into dyspnea and can't breathe, is that below the standard of care for malpractice?

Incredibly, this author has had cases such as this in which the hired guns of the court (medical expert witnesses for sale) have argued and testified both ways.

In one such case, a twenty-three-year-old mother of two had such an incident happen to her. The doctor hired an expert to say this was not malpractice because it was "an unforeseeable injury." An expert was hired by the mother's attorney (this author) who said the opposite. Ultimately, the case was settled with a result beneficial to the mother. This is an example of Newton's Second Law of the Law, "for every expert witness opinion, there is an equal and opposite expert witness opinion."

Who is right?

Perhaps God alone can decide that.

But since we are a nation of people and not Gods, the fact is that there is no correct or certain opinion. Newton's Second Law of the Law clearly injects a massive degree of uncertainty into the equation, permitting the debtor to battle the medical creditor by asserting malpractice as a defense to any credit collection attempt.

Once the "guilty" doctor's collection juggernaut has sprung into action, the debtor-patient can fight back by asserting a malpractice claim as a defense. He can assert that the doctor was "negligent" and "fell below the standard of professional care in the area," and refuse to pay his bill.

The wise debtor will then launch a preemptive strike against the medical service by filing a malpractice suit, or at least threatening to do so, to ward off the collection monster.

Given the uncertainty of the law, there is a good chance that the collector will just give up, write off the debt as uncollectible, and walk away. Even if the creditor sues, he can be dragged through the quicksand of the court system for years, as the debtor's insertion of a countersuit for malpractice can complicate the issue and result in a massive discovery war. This will most likely become so expensive to the doctor that he will wind up paying more money to lawyers than he could ever possibly collect. In addition, he will run the risk of jeopardizing his medical license, since state medical licensing boards are typically interested in any malpractice case filed against an M.D. and will discipline the doctor. If the trial verdict is above some minimum dollar amount, automatic reporting requirements kick in that will alert state licensing medical boards of the case. In California, the minimum threshold for such reporting requirements is $30,000.

The debtor can also launch a peripheral attack against the doctor by filing a complaint with the state licensing board, the better business bureau, the local medical society, etc.

All of these tactics serve to damage the doctor's reputation, and jeopardize his license, so that the "rational medical player" will run away like a wet poodle, with his tail between his legs, rather than pursue a futile and self-damaging collection war in the courts.

THE EXPERT WITNESS: THE SECRET WEAPON OF THE COUNTERSUIT

Now for the coup de grace in this medical collection gambit: Those wanting to combat a medical collector do not even need to find the support of a medical expert witness. The popular folk wisdom is that doctors will not testify against other doctors. The implication is that any potential lawsuit against a doctor will be cut off at the knees and cannot even get started. This is a widely held fallacy because it is only at the proverbial end of the game, when the two-minute warning has been given, that the medical expert must be produced to satisfy the technical demands of going to court.

Why is this?

Although most states (whose legislator puppets are generally controlled by the rapid-dispenser-of-campaign-cash medical industry) now have laws on the books requiring the debtors to "certify" in a letter to the doctor, ninety days before suing for malpractice, that they have an expert witness supporting their theory of malpractice. In practice, this is a meaningless and unenforceable rule.

Anyone can meet this pseudo-requirement by hiring an expert-for-sale from a directory of experts. The idea that doctors will not testify against other doctors has been reduced to a gross canard by now. The truth is there is an entire sub-industry of doctors who do nothing but provide the service of testifying at trials. The old premise was based on the concept that a doctor would have some sort of difficulty when he returned to regular practice after having testified against one of his colleagues. But of course the professional expert does not return to regular practice. He has his new profession as an expert witness and makes his living hanging doctors out to dry. We have reached the point where medical lawsuits are as common as medical horror stories and each of them has an expert witness (or several). Usually, the doctor who will testify against another doctor is as close as the phone book.

At the early stages of the lawsuit, however, all that is necessary can be obtained by consulting any doctor and getting even the slightest nod toward an opinion that would constitute an endorsement for a malpractice claim.

The expert witness supporting the malpractice theory need not be "disclosed" in the lawsuit until nearly the end of the game. This typically comes thirty to sixty days before trial, and by that time, chances are that the medical collector will have already given up and settled the case.

The inherent uncertainty and chicanery behind so much of medical malpractice law can be seen in the 1982 Paul Newman movie *The Verdict*. Watching this movie is a must for any debtor seeking to play this "malpractice" card to avoid medical provider debt.

CASTING A WIDE NET OVER THE MEDICAL ESTABLISHMENT

Malpractice cases can be filed not only against individual doctors, but also against hospitals, medical centers, medical labs, nurses, nurses' aides, orderlies, and the like. Because of the "law of accountability" (the technical term is the doctrine of *respondeat superior*), all of these entities are liable for the mistake of a single person down the chain of command. This does not even begin to address the whole world of anesthesiologists, various specialists, suppliers of defective medical products, and pharmaceutical companies who may be liable or partially liable when they are involved in circumstances that lead to harming a patient.

All it takes is the will and the commitment to see it through for the debtor-patient to assert his rights by filing a malpractice claim.

One stumbling block to be aware of here is the statute of limitations for malpractice suits, which vary from state to state. Generally the longest, often as long as six years, are found in the eastern United States. The shortest limitation periods within which to file suit are in the West, where it may be only one year. If the collection agency/doctor waits for the statute of limitations to run out before suing the debtor for costs owed, it will be too late for the debtor to file a countersuit for malpractice, because the statute of limitations will have run out.

It should not be surprising that most states provide a much longer statute of limitations for allowing creditors to sue debtors than for the period within which to sue under a malpractice cause of action. This is again a result of the "Puppet Law of the Law." The legislators who pass these statute of limitations laws are typically puppets of a medical industry that is a cash cow for campaign funds. This is why the wise debtor will check his statute of limitations and will strike first by filing the malpractice suit before he is sued for money owed.

But even if the statute of limitations has run out for malpractice suits, the debtor can take heart. Most "common law" courts allow the debtor to assert a malpractice claim as an "offset" defense to a collection lawsuit. That is, even after the statute of limitations for malpractice has run out, if the debtor is later sued by the doctor, he can still assert as a defense the "offset" theory that the doctor, committed malpractice and thus damaged him to the amount of umpteen dollars. This little-known fact is a powerful weapon in the debtor's arsenal.

Medicine in the United States is part of a corporate structure that is generally concerned only with the bottom line, which usually means, "Deliver the least amount of care for the least cost." These days, HMOs are largely in charge of delivering health care, and it is usually quite easy to find an act of medical malpractice or malfeasance in these entities' decisions on patient care, because the mighty green buck takes precedence over the less powerful red blood. If any conceivable medical test was not performed to properly diagnose a condition, there is a potential for a counterclaim or lawsuit against the provider, for malpractice. Many of these tests are expensive, such as the MRI, the CT SCAN, biopsies, exploratory surgery, and the like. As such, HMOs are likely to balk at the prospect of paying for the tests, and the tests are likely to be omitted.

Six months later, when an ignored lump turns out to be cancer or some other dreaded disease, the debtor can claim "malpractice" against the doctor.

In these Doctor vs. Debtor Wars, the Debtor is almost always likely to prevail, because no doctor is perfect and because anything less than absolute perfection can constitute malpractice.

Rather than face a lengthy, embarrassing lawsuit and risk damage to reputation and bad publicity, doctors and HMOs and hospitals are likely to settle for pennies on the dollar, or to write off the debt entirely.

ARBITRATION:
QUICKSAND OF THE "MED MAL" GAME

Because doctors fear malpractice so much, they have increasingly sought to insulate themselves from the threat of "Med Mal" suits by forcing all patients to sign away their rights to sue in court, in advance of receiving medical treatment, and requiring them to limit their remedy for "all disputes over treatment" to that dreaded bugaboo, arbitration ("Arb").

Arbitration is the "quicksand" of the debt wars, because it seems to take away much of the debtor-litigant's arsenal of expensive and hard-hitting tools, and because "Arb" usually results in a patsy posing as "neutral arbiter," when in fact the patsy is generally controlled by the doctor.

But all is not lost! All the debtor has to do to bypass the arbitration slough of quicksand is to file a lawsuit in court accusing the doctor of "fraud in the inducement of my signature on the arbitration agreement."

"Fraud" is analogous to the joker in a deck of cards. It enables the debtor-litigant to get around the arbitration trap by alleging that the doctor forced him to sign the mandatory Arb Agreement by making false promises, inducing his reliance thereon.

One of the most pernicious practitioners of the Arb Gambit is that trusty McDonald's of medical organizations, Kaiser Permanente. Kaiser routinely undercuts the competition by offering patients typically low premium rates. Like its counterpart in the fast food realm, this "McHospital" tends to attract blue-collar workers and other debtors barely able to make ends meet.

It is a Kaiser policy to require every patient to sign away his rights, before getting any treatment, by agreeing not to sue for malpractice in court for a future act of malpractice, and by agreeing to arbitrate any dispute through what is called "binding arbitration." This means that the patient and McHospital brass will agree on an arbitrator or arbitrators, from a list controlled generally by McHospital, and that the arbitrator's decision will be absolutely binding and impossible to appeal.

Now, what Kaiser (and its analogues) fail to tell the patient is that Kaiser itself "administers" its arbitration "program," which means that it controls the agenda, provides lists of pseudo-neutral arbitrators, collects the fees, and decides the ground rules for the Arb Game.

Because this fact is never disclosed to patients, courts have often found fraud in the inducement of the agreement, and have allowed the patient to bypass the Arb quicksand and fight his battle in the terra firma of the courtroom.

But for those debtors unwilling or unable to play the fraud card, arbitration is the killing field of all malpractice cases. Studies have shown that nearly 90 percent of all arbitration decisions have been rendered in favor of the entity that administers the program. Kaiser won the prize in 88 percent of its cases. That is typical of McHospitals across the country.

Why is the figure so high? How can this be fair?

Arbitrators are generally retired judges, retired or active lawyers, and others who realize that to make a successful and lucrative career out of arbitration, they must play the tune dictated by the McHospital.

The McHospital will ruthlessly cut from its stable of arbitrator ponies anyone who dares to rule against it. Because the McHospital controls 99 percent of the information concerning the background and track record of its arbitrator shills, it is able to keep this information secret. Kaiser, for example, typically runs 10,000 malpractice arbitrations each year, often using the same arbitrator stable ponies over and over again.

By contrast, Joe Patient is typically running blind and nervous, on his first and only arbitration. Is it any wonder that McHospital usually wins the arbitration game?

I have seen patients who suffered egregious acts of malpractice, and who then sank in the quicksand of arbitration. One patient was victimized by a McHospital doctor who left a surgical clip on his ureter. The clip caused permanent damage to the kidney, which required three more "repair" operations. In the last one, the doctor unnecessarily removed the patient's kidney without even getting his consent. The case went to "mandatory arbitration," and the arbitrator ruled in favor of the McHospital doctor. The case was never reported to the state medical board or to the malpractice insurer. Then the patient succumbed to kidney failure three months later, and died. His spouse tried to sue the McHospital for wrongful death in court, but was quickly derailed into "mandatory arbitration." The court ruled that under the Arb Agreement, she was bound by her husband's decision to opt for mandatory arbitration.

In another case, a woman going into McHospital for a routine childbirth woke up to find that a hysterectomy has been performed—again without her consent. She was railroaded into a futile and hopeless Arb session and lost.

If McHospitals can win easy arbitrations like this, what cases can't they win?

Another reason why the McHospitals win the arbitration game so often is that the cost of arbitration "fixed fees" is so high that the patient is manipulated and bullied out of the game.

While the cost of filing a lawsuit in court is generally only about $200 in any court in the country, the cost of paying an arbitrator is $5,000 on average. This means that a patient who suffered the amputation of the "wrong arm" will have to pony up $5,000 cash just to get into the Arb arena and play the game. (Even if a patient-litigant finds a lawyer willing to take his case "on contingency fee," he will still have to pay all costs up front, including arbitrator fees and expert witness fees).

Typically, Arb Meisters like Kaiser exploit this charade by offering to pay all arbitration fees if the patient agrees to have only one arbitrator, rather than three. What patient can resist such a bribe? Yet statistics show that a patient's chances of winning with one arbitrator is vastly lower than his chances of winning with three.

To go through a full-scale arbitration with three arbitrators, each charging an average of $5,000, a patient would have to borrow heavily or exhaust all of his savings. Then, on top of that, he would have to pay another $10,000 to hire his own expert witness for the Arb hearing, for it is impossible to win a malpractice case without an expert witness. He may find it very difficult, or impossible, to find a local doctor willing to testify against a colleague. So he must pay a premium fee to find another doctor witness-for-hire in another state or faraway city, plus heavy-duty travel and hotel expenses, easily exceeding $10,000 to stay in the game. Because most people cannot afford these rates, which may exceed even their damages, they are likely to fold, and the entire game is likely to peter out in the early innings before the patient even gets to bat.

With such a system, is it any wonder why the Arb game is the quicksand of all debtors?

To leapfrog over this quicksand, the debtor-patient must be prepared to play the fraud card, that is to allege fraud in the inducement of the Arb agreement, and march straight to court.

THE LAW OF SUPPLY AND
DEMAND: STUDENT LOANS

WE ALL KNOW that colleges and universities in this country have massively hiked up their tuition, room, and board costs over the past twenty years. It has reached the point where all but the most wealthy students must take out massive student loans in order to get through school, particularly private schools.

It is not uncommon for an undergraduate to emerge from four long years of toil with a sheepskin in one hand and a student loan debt of $50,000 in the other.

For graduate and professional school, the final tally is even worse; the average graduate of medical or law school owes $120,000 to creditors, "guaranteed" by Uncle Sam.

In short, it is estimated that every freshly minted lawyer and doctor in this country will spend the first five years of work just paying off those massive student loans.

Does it have to be that way?

DEBUNKING THE GREAT MYTH
OF STUDENT LOANS

Among the great myths of our time is that "student loans cannot be avoided." Almost all students believe that once they get their degrees, they will have no choice but to pay off the debt to their creditors. If they do not pay, they will be hauled before a debtor's court, sued by the mighty federal government itself (as guarantor of all student loans), and forced to do penance, lose all their assets and licenses, and descend into ignominy.

Even bankruptcy has been removed by Congress as a way out of paying student loans. Like income taxes, student loan debtors cannot walk away from their debt by filing for bankruptcy protection.

Let us bypass for a moment the ethics of stiffing student loan creditors. I will also bypass for the moment the fact that colleges are supposed to be "nonprofit" charitable institutions dedicated to the scholar's light rather than the merchant's bank account. These are subjects that can and should be addressed in student-debtor lawsuits against the lending institution and its college partners.

It should be said at the outset that the myth of inevitability of student loan payment is like all other myths at core—false, deceptive, and without a basis in reality.

How can a medical student get out of paying back $120,000 to Uncle Sam and the bank that financed his sojourn through the halls of academia? The first thing to recognize about student loans is that they are, in essence, no different than any other kind of loan or debt. They still obey the same laws of the law, the same economic realities, and the same laws of flexibility.

Whether your creditor is an unshaven and unscrupulous snake oil salesman or a pinstriped Ivy League aristocrat, the realities of the law still apply. Yes, you can get out of paying a penny in student loans, or paying no more than a dime on the dollar. How so?

The only difference between student loans and other types of garden-variety debt is that the former cannot be discharged by bankruptcy. Since we have already shown why bankruptcy is the worst possible form of debt avoidance available, this really makes no difference, since the prudent debtor will not go the bankruptcy route anyway.

Now, you say, "But Uncle Sam lies behind the student loan scams, waiting to pounce on debtors with the full might of the federal government." Yes, but take a look for a moment at what the federal government is. The United States federal government is the most shameless, inefficient, and incompetent debtor in history.

Since 1969, the federal budget has been in debt for all but three years, which means it has been in the red for 90 percent of the time. Today, even the will-o'-the-wisp Clinton-era budget surpluses have given way to more reckless profligacy in spending by the Bush Administration.

Can anyone seriously look at this player, Uncle Sam, and shrink in fear that such a reckless spendthrift will seriously enforce student loan debts owed by Joe Debtor?

In other words, federal bureaucrats entrusted with collecting student loans are operating under the embarrassing fact that they themselves are a part of a machine that has run up huge oceans of debt without blinking an eye.

THE UNFULFILLED PROMISE OF EDUCATION

To avoid paying back student loans one need only look at the most elemental aspects of what the school originally promised, and then failed to deliver.

There was a time when Ivy League college recruiters lured a student to their institutions by promising the moon and the stars. They promised a great job, a great career, and a great title. But how many of those promises were not fulfilled?

College recruiters and administrators are prone to resorting to puffery, hyperbole, and the like to recruit students. Because a college's main aim in life is to collect money, it has to resort to these cutthroat business practices in order to lure a student to its hallowed yards and quadrangles, lest another school get him (and his wallet) first.

Harvard, which claims to be a "nonprofit university," has an "endowment" of more than $15 billion, which is more than even the federal government itself can claim to have. Yet, it claims it "needs" to collect student fees (the rate of return on Harvard's endowment is so staggeringly great that every year, the money sitting idle earns so much that the endowment doubles every five years).

Because colleges are essentially *for-profit* entities, despite their denials to the contrary, they can be sued and countersued as much as one pleases.

In a lawsuit for fraud and breach of contract, one of the most powerful legal theories to present at court is the theory that the school failed to deliver what it had promised the debtor, namely a great job and career. In litigation, especially for the nationally known schools, the debtor-litigants can demand copious information about every alumnus and student since the college opened its doors to show discrimination, a pattern of lies, and so on. Few colleges are foolhardy enough to waste their resources chasing a student debtor. Even the redoubtable Harvard University, they of the multi-billion endowment fame, has proved to be a paper tiger when engaged in litigation.

10

TAX WARS AND GRUNTS: BATTLING THE IRS

THINKING ABOUT LINCOLN and what he stood for and against, it is ironic that the first federal income tax was levied during the Civil War—a temporary and very small tax to be sure, but the tax that broke the ice.

Today, Lincoln's idea of a temporary ad hoc tax to support a Civil War has ballooned into a massive permanent bureaucracy that is surely the most unpopular agency in the government. Forcing taxpayers to pony up regular money to the government—money the government did not earn—has become a massive business.

Most people believe that the IRS is absolutely omnipotent, and that there is no way to battle the IRS in court or to even raise a finger in protest at being ripped off by a government that really has no legitimate right to take people's hard-earned money as taxes.

What happens when Uncle Sam comes calling in the form of your friendly IRS? What do you do?

Millions of people regularly cheat on their tax returns, by not reporting income "under the table," by running up bogus and dubious costs and expenditures, by seeking tax shelters and the like. Yet for every man, woman, and child, there is a Tax Man waiting in the wings, eager to swoop down and pounce on the taxpayer.

First of all, for those adventurous souls who feel they have discovered a great idea in alleging that the U.S. tax system is "unconstitutional," forget it. Attempting to challenge the constitutionality of the U.S. tax system in court has already been done umpteen times, by umpteen angry, revolting taxpayers. The income tax has been upheld because of the 16th Amendment to the U.S. Constitution, which was enacted in 1913.

Second, if you want to challenge the IRS seriously as a debtor, take them to court on the issues at hand in *your* specific case. Like any other creditor, the IRS is amenable to settling cases for less than 100 percent, in order to obviate litigation.

THE IRS IN U.S. TAX COURT

There are two types of courts where the debtor taxpayer can seek justice and a compromise: U.S. tax court and U.S. district court.

First, let us consider the U.S. tax court. If the IRS issues a ninety-day deficiency notice, informing the taxpayer that his tax return has been scrutinized and that he has been found wanting and that he must pay money to the IRS, the taxpayer can file an action in U.S. tax court to challenge the Notice of Deficiency. This action will tie up the matter for years.

This writer handled a case for a millionaire taxpayer who managed to tie up the IRS for twelve years, arguing over $12 million allegedly due on taxes. The endless stratagems available to a taxpayer-litigant can hold off the IRS wolves for quite a long time.

THE IRS IN U.S. DISTRICT COURT

If the taxpayer elects to pay the taxes, he can still dispute them by filing a different kind of action in U.S. district court. The disadvantage of this choice is that it is necessary to pay all the money the IRS demands as a precondition of filing the suit. The advantage is once the tax is paid, interest on the unpaid balance does not accumulate during the lawsuit. By contrast, interest will continue to accumulate for any unpaid taxes while a taxpayer sues the IRS in U.S. tax court.

Tax law is indeed esoteric and ridiculously complex. A whole library can be filled by the tomes and volumes of "IRS Rules and Regulations," which the IRS itself prints in order to interpret its own tax code. The tax code itself is so riddled with contradictory provisions and ambiguous terminology that a determined taxpayer can drag out the battle of interpretations for years. The ambiguity is often deliberately injected into the stew of words cooked up by the Congress, in order to satisfy all disparate sides and thereby get the tax bill enacted via coalition voting.

THE TAX LAW AS THE TOOL OF POLITICIANS

This writer once worked in the U.S. Senate and was amazed to observe the huge lines of business lobbyists lined up daily to chit-chat with Senators on the Finance Committee, which was responsible for writing the tax code. In general, translated into practical terms, this meant that for every dollar a lobbyist gave an elected official, the individuals or groups that the lobbyists represented could expect savings of at least $3 on a tax bill. This was accomplished by the politicians carving out exceptions to obscure code sections and subsections that would match the situation of the interested parties.

Some of the exceptions were shamefully obvious, as in a 1980s' tax bill that amended the tax code and specifically exempted in the words of the law "a certain corporation in Decatur, Illinois." This "certain corporation" was Archer Daniels Midland (ADM), the food agribusiness giant whose chairman,

Dwayne Andreas, was one of the top campaign contributors to the then–Senate Finance Committee Chairman, Bob Dole.

Of course, the average Joe Q. Taxpayer is in no position to pony up millions of dollars in campaign cash to the politicians-for-sale, and, of course, the average Joe Q. Debtor is in even worse shape. As a result, he is stuck as a "grunt bearing the brunt" of the hideously unfair and oppressive U.S. tax code.

We have all heard of corporations who have created "off-shore tax shelters" by setting up an office with a phone in the Bahamas or some Caribbean island, and thereby manage to legally evaded paying any taxes whatsoever to Uncle Sam. It is these same corporate swindlers who wave the flag and claim to be "patriots" at the political dinners where the political parties and candidates raise their millions.

During the Vietnam War, it was well known that the G.I. "grunts" sent into battle were generally poor or working-class people, while the scions of the rich and well-to-do escaped the draft by enrolling in expensive colleges.

Similarly, in the Tax Wars, the "grunts" who are forced to bear the brunt of the tax burden are average people. Studies show that IRS auditors have gone after grunts with a vengeance, while routinely letting huge cash cows of campaign fundraising like Enron and WorldCom go unaudited.

What fairness can there be in such a system? With what moral authority can the IRS dare to go after Joe Q. Taxpayer?

Any expectation that the IRS and the big government agencies that feed upon it are going to sit around debating metaphysical theories of fairness will be sorely disappointed. The IRS is a well-tuned machine, the tank corps of the government tax army. It is ready for combat, and its enemy is the common grunt in the trenches, namely you and me.

So what can the grunt do?

The Answer Is Simple: Sue, Sue, Sue

By refusing to pay the tax and challenging the legitimacy of the IRS's decision to levy taxes, and by filing his court action in the U.S. tax courts, the grunt can hold off the IRS for years. In the end, he can negotiate an offer to settle the tax liability for a far smaller sum than demanded by the bad guys.

Based on the principles enunciated in this book, and on Newton's Laws and the other laws mentioned, there is an excellent chance that Joe Q. Taxpayer can win or, at least, negotiate an advantageous settlement. Indeed, if there were enough Joe Q. Taxpayers out there who mobilized and filed actions in federal court against the IRS en masse, they could shut the system down. No one would really want that result, of course, but an understanding of that possibility by the government—as well as by the readers of this book—gives the informed and aggressive taxpayer a lot of power.

If a case filed in court against the IRS ever went to trial before a jury of one's peers, rest assured that the IRS would be in hot water. "Everybody hates the IRS" is a maxim everyone knows. Any red-blooded American juror, faced with a chance to "stick it to 'em" in retaliation for all the wrongs the IRS has done to him over the years, will seize the moment and vote against the dreaded "Service."

This is the secret that the IRS never wants the average taxpayer to discover and the IRS itself never wants put to the test: Actually going the distance and taking a court case all the way into a jury trial would test the very basis of the tax collection system. Almost everyone assumes—even the IRS itself—that the IRS would almost always lose.

I have seen this principle in action, time and again. One of my clients, a former IRS employee who was wrongly discharged and then sued the Service, won a massive verdict. Afterwards, jurors interviewed said they were disgusted with the IRS's "arrogance . . . chicanery . . . greed . . . heavy-handed tactics."

Who indeed could not empathize with the litigant suing the dreaded beast of all collectors? Who among us would seriously vote for an agency that everyone knows is unfair and prejudiced in its singular pursuit of the average helpless citizen, while letting the high-and-mighty corporate criminals and tax frauds escape unscathed with a handshake from the President in front of the White House?

Yes, tax collectors are among the vilest of all creditors, and are far more powerful. They can shut down a business, padlock the doors, and seize the assets of a business without trial or lawsuit. They have the authority to do this and will do it unless the taxpayer strikes first by filing suit. Once the magic bullet is fired, once suit is filed in federal court, the IRS is automatically restrained. The taxpayer can file a "motion for protective order" with the court, asking that the IRS be enjoined from taking any collection activities while the case is pending. Generally, judges grant such orders. The IRS Minotaur knows that it can thrive only by brutally gobbling up undefended taxpayers in the Labyrinth of the tax code. It will focus its energies on them and devour them if unrestrained by an action in court.

11

"HOUSEJACKERS, BEWARE!"

OF ALL THE THREATS POSED by creditors, the most serious is that of "taking over the debtor's house." With the rise of home-lessness over the past twenty years, with scare stories multiply-ing like rabbits out of the hat, polls show that Americans fear losing their homes more than nearly anything else.

The idea that a ruthless creditor can just simply march into court like a bull charging into a ring, file a few documents, and then foreclose on one's home—one's castle—is a deep-rooted fear.

SAVING ONE'S HOUSE:
THE FIRST LINE OF DEFENSE

Fear of losing one's home—of being "housejacked"—comes not only from fear of the mortgage company that has stuck its talons into one's home by means of "deeds of trust" and "liens." It also comes from standard garden-variety creditors, like Visa or MasterCard companies, which delight in waving the "Housejacker" boogeyman before frightened debtors.

Yet if one plays his cards correctly, fear of being house-jacked need not be of major concern. The law in this country, which since the days of the Founding Fathers has always protected property far more than individuals, has imbedded so many legal safeguards and twists and turns in the labyrinth of debt collection litigation, that a clever homeowner can shield himself from housejacking, no matter what the numbers.

There is the first line of defense, the "homestead exemption." Surprisingly few debtors know of the availability of this shield, yet it is as old as the Constitution itself. Every state has its own homestead exemption. For example, in Arizona and in Massachusetts the Homestead Exemption is $100,000; in North Dakota it is $80,000.

In each state, any homeowner can shield his house from predator-creditors to the extent of the statutory "exemption," by simply recording a document called "Declaration of Homestead," in the county recorder's office. The standard fee in the recorder's office is about $20. This declaration serves to put creditors and the world on notice that the homeowner lives in the property in question and is claiming it as his homestead. The law says you are protected to the extent of the exemption, which should exceed the equity of the debtor in the house— thus making the debtor "judgment proof" as far as his home is concerned.

Apart from the homestead declaration, the real question is: How does one defend against a mortgage company or lien holder who places a lien on a house and seeks to force a sale or to foreclose on the house?

THE THREE TYPES OF LENDERS WHO WANT YOUR HOME

Moneylenders who might seek to force a borrower from his home fall into three major categories. First is the legitimate garden-variety garter snake, such as your friendly bank. The second is the rattlesnake or so-called "hard money lender" who charges you a premium high interest rate to take out "high-risk loans." These snakes are highly dangerous because they are not interested in the standard return and make their real money from taking possession of your collateral.

The third type of lender is the boa constrictor, that is, actual loan sharks who charge exorbitant, usurious rates and break your legs if you do not pay up. It is to be hoped that no one is ever desperate enough to borrow from that sort of lender, and if you do end up on bad terms with the local "Godfather," your problems may be beyond the scope of this book.

Of these three types of lenders, the first is the most difficult to defend against. But, as in all things legal, there is always a loophole out of the mortgage contract. There is always a way to stave off the creditor zombies.

READ THE FINE PRINT, READ THE LAW

The basic defense against garter-snake lenders is to assert breach of contract and fraud, both in the manner in which the loan was first secured and negotiated, and in the manner in which foreclosure notices were sent. All states have stringent laws concerning notice requirements for a lender to foreclose on a residential or commercial loan.

Amazingly few lenders follow these rules by the letter, because they know that 99 percent of all debtors in default are not going to bother to fight the foreclosure.

The laws vary from state to state, and the debtor should look in the state codes to determine which state laws apply. Some states call their codes by a name, such as the "California Civil Code," which covers real property laws. Other states call their codes by generic numbers, such as "Massachusetts General Statutes Volume IX." It is easy to look up laws by starting with the index of the code. The same can be done online at Internet legal research sites.

In addition to state laws, there are federal laws that govern mortgage lending. Federal laws often conflict with particular state laws, and this contradiction creates a seed that can germinate into a massive lawsuit or countersuit against the lender.

Federal laws are codified in 50 titles of the U.S. Code. Each title represents a subject area. For example, title 42 concerns civil rights and government aid statutes; title 17 concerns copyrights; title 18 is the federal criminal code; title 26 is the internal revenue (tax) code, and so on.

Just look in the index to the entire code and you will be led to the right section.

A wise debtor technically "in default" on a mortgage can easily tie up his creditor for years by suing him in both federal and state court, alleging fraud and breach of contract as well as violations of technical statutory provisions.

One of the most fruitful fields in which to grow an anti-mortgage lawsuit is that of the reams of forms presented to the borrower when he signs up for the loan. Usually, lenders and their title company officers treat the massive form requirements in a rote and cursory manner, handing the debtor hundreds of pages of small print, not giving him enough time to seriously review the documents, and assuring the debtor that all is okay, that he should trust the lender.

Few borrowers read the forms. Studies show that only one in fifty borrowers even try to read the prolix and tedious material, and of those, less than 20 percent bother to read all.

Lenders know this and therefore often sneak in provisions never fully explained to the borrower. In an anti-mortgage suit or countersuit, the clever debtor-litigant will seize upon this and accuse the lender of deliberate misrepresentation and concealment of key facts contained in the fine print of some of these forms.

Maybe You Didn't Sign Your Life Away

If the lender (or title company proffering the forms to the borrower) failed to give the borrower sufficient time to read the forms, and handed them to him at 6:30 P.M. on a Friday afternoon, and pressured him to sign them without reading them, there are grounds for challenging the entire loan transaction in court. The mere fact that a debtor has signed a form does not *ipso facto* mean that he is bound by what he purportedly signed.

This principle, that "to sign is not to sign," is what might be called the "Heisenberg Uncertainty Principle of the Law."

In the 1920s, physicist Werner Heisenberg enunciated his famous "Uncertainty Principle," which held that "it is impossible to determine with absolute certainty exactly what an elementary particle's position and momentum are, at the same time." The physical nature of the universe, and particularly the tenuous nature of physical laws as they apply to elementary particles like atoms and electrons and protons, can also be translated in the law as a crucial and salient law in itself.

Heisenberg's Uncertainty Principle of the Law maintains that "it is never certain whether a person who signed a legal document had actually read it and comprehended it before signing it." That is, the mere fact of a signature on a form does not necessarily make this a binding contract. Because contract law in every state and federal court holds that in order for a contract to be valid and binding, there must be a "mutual meeting of the minds" between both parties, one can always assert that he or she did not read or understand the forms he or she has signed. The debtor can invoke Heisenberg's Uncertainty Principle to nullify the very mortgage contract upon which the creditors seek to foreclose on his property.

The Heisenberg Uncertainty Principle can be applied against any of the three types of creditors mentioned above. It is easiest to assert against loan sharks and hard money lenders, particularly since they usually engage in heavy-handed tactics to con the debtor into signing on the dotted line of about 300 pages, in ten minutes or fewer. But the principle can also be applied against a conventional bank or mortgage company.

Once you assert, in a lawsuit or countersuit, that you did not read or understand the forms you signed to get the loan, you magically open a Pandora's box. You invoke the Uncertainty Principle.

That means that you can litigate this issue for years, wearing down the lender and prodding him toward a compromise. For example, lenders will often back down from their truculent "steamroller" mentality by renegotiating or refinancing the loan, sharply reducing the monthly payments, and forgetting about defaults and foreclosures. They will thus change the terms of the loan in order to avoid a lengthy and expensive lawsuit.

MOSES' LAW OF THE LAW: NOTHING IS WRITTEN IN STONE

A great religious and historical figure, Moses, provides us with yet another trenchant and valuable law. I call this "Moses' Law of the Law," and it holds that "In the Law, nothing is written in stone, except God's Ten Commandments."

In the 1940s, there was a movie called *The Devil and Daniel Webster,* in which a poor farmer sells his soul to the devil by signing his name in blood, promising to proffer his soul as a quid pro quo for a massive "loan" of money. Old Daniel Webster, the famous lawyer and U.S. Senator from New Hampshire, applied "Moses' Law of the Law" and argued against the devil before a jury, insisting eloquently that "nothing man writes is written in stone." A poor man who had been "misled" by the devil into signing away his soul should not and could not be held literally to his pledge. Although the farmer had received the Golden Calf of Riches (via a "loan"), Webster argued that he should not be forced to keep up his end of the bargain. Webster was particularly brilliant in appealing to the jury's emotions and in urging them to put themselves in the farmer's place: "Who among you would not want a Second Chance?" he asked.

The jury, though comprised of corrupt men, agreed with Webster and exonerated the farmer, who was then allowed to live out his life without having to give up his soul—or to pay back the loan.

There are always loopholes and ways to get out of a contract, and it is simply up to the wise debtor to find them. Sometimes, the debtor has to search for one honest witness to back up his claims that he did not understand what he signed over to the devil. At other times, he must revert to his personal documents, ledgers, and journals written at the time he signed the contract, to prove his defense of ignorance and misunderstanding. But always, he will find a way out.

KIPLING'S LAW OF THE LAW: PLAYING THE PR CARD

In the area of home foreclosures, one must also be willing and able to play the "PR Card," which might be called "Kipling's Law of the Law."

Rudyard Kipling, the immortal British author, coined a rejoinder to the saying that "Blood is thicker than water" when he said that, "Ink is thicker than blood." What he meant by this maxim was that if a libelous or harshly negative statement about a person or company appeared in print, it would prove to be far more powerful than the "truth."

Translated into modern day lingo, Kipling's Law of the Law means that if a harshly condemnatory story about a creditor appears in the newspaper or television, the indelible image created by that "ink" can serve to negate the bonds created by a mere "blood" signature on a contract.

Mortgage companies and lenders are generally very sensitive to bad publicity, because they know that their business depends largely on maintaining a good public image. Thus, if one borrower goes to the media and convinces them to publicize a particularly unfair mortgage foreclosure, the chances are that the lenders will cringe and retreat . . . if the media campaign is handled competently.

I have seen Kipling's Law of the Law in operation so many times that it is almost laughable how easily creditors will back down in the face of public pressure. In recent years, it has become far easier to put Kipling's Law into effect because of the wide proliferation of mass media, the Internet, and the transformation of "evening news" programs into "entertainment venues." Additionally, because there are more and more lenders appearing on the market every day, bombarding people with unsolicited e-mail and actual mail peddling mortgage giveaways, every lender faces stiffer competition for loans daily.

A few years ago, an old widow in Oakland, California, faced seemingly certain foreclosure on her home of fifty years. The story that soon came out in the news media, on every local news show, was that a "sharp-practicing" hard money lender had conned her into signing away her rights to her home by inserting a cleverly concealed "balloon payment provision" in her mortgage contract. The balloon payment provision (which, by the way, is very common in mortgages written by hard money lenders and loan sharks) provided that after the fifth year of the loan, $200,000 would be due in ten days, on pain of foreclosure.

The widow had never understood this language, not being trained in the law. With the help of a lawyer, she was able to hold onto her home by breaking the back of the loan shark. By exposing these shenanigans in all the local news broadcasts and the newspapers, and by suing the bad guy for fraud and breach of contract and violation of a plethora of federal and state consumer protection statutes, the lender was portrayed as the epitome of fraud and deceit, a callous Scrooge and a scoundrel. People were urged to boycott the lender, and soon, hundreds of other befuddled borrowers came forth with similar tales. The widow kept her house, and she forced the bad guy to renegotiate the terms of the loan.

What has been said above as to mortgage foreclosures applies even more strongly to those creditors who obtain a "lien" on a debtor's house by getting a court judgment against him, and who then threaten to force a sale of the house to satisfy the judgment.

In addition to smearing the lender with bad publicity, a wise debtor will countersue the bad guy in court, alleging fraud, breach of contract, discrimination, violation of consumer protection laws, and more.

Now, what about the creditor who tries to take your house by suing you on an unsecured debt (a debt other than a mortgage), and winning a judgment against you? How do you fight this type of dragon?

In virtually all states, a creditor who sues a debtor on an "unsecured" loan in a lawsuit unrelated to a mortgage default, and who wins a judgment against the debtor in court, can then get a "lien" against the debtor's property, including his home. In theory, the creditor can then petition the court to order a "forced sale" of the debtor's home, to extract his pound of flesh to pay off the judgment.

In theory, if a debtor owns a home worth $500,000 and has equity of $200,000 in it, with a homestead declaration on file where the limit is $100,000, and if the creditor's judgment is for $10,000, the creditor can force a sale of the home, throw the debtor out on the street, and hand him only his exemption amount.

Of course, this gambit of "forced sale" is rarely used in practice, but unscrupulous and ruthless creditors will often threaten it as a scare tactic to force the debtor to either sell his home, refinance it, or to otherwise act to come up with the cash.

The wise debtor will, of course, tie the creditor up in the courts for years with a complaint against the underlying transaction to prevent him from obtaining a judgment leading to a lien. But if that fails, or if the debtor comes into "Debtor Consciousness" late in the game—after a judgment lien has been attached to the property—there is still hope!

A forced sale petition is not a sure thing in any state. Most states have tons of loopholes in the law, enabling the well-versed debtor to escape from the clutches of his oppressor by alleging "hardship," financial burden, or a gross disparity between the amount of the judgment and the equity in the home.

In most states, judges are elected and are up for re-election every few years. They too obey Kipling's Law of the Law, in that they do not wish to antagonize voters by "throwing a family out on the street" in order to satisfy some greedy corporation, particularly a faceless, out-of-state corporation.

The wise debtor then will invoke Kipling's Law and will head for the "PR Portal," and will try to interest news reporters and television and radio stations into publicizing the unfair and outrageous oppressive actions of the greedy creditors.

Most voters have an instinctive sense of "justice" and react sharply to charges of "unfairness" and "oppressiveness." Judges are sensitive to bad PR and will generally refrain from granting a petition to force the sale of a home to satisfy a relatively small judgment, or even a large judgment, particularly if a Homestead Declaration is on file at the county recorder's office.

If the amount of the judgment is large, and proportional to the amount of equity, a debtor may be in more trouble. Still, the debtor can play his poker hand wisely and dodge the bullet of the forced sale.

"DILUTING EQUITY" AS A
SHIELD AGAINST CREDITORS

In ancient Rome, where our legal system actually began, an anonymous wit came up with a theory. In modern terms, it holds that "The less equity one has in his property, the less vulnerable the property is to seizure, and the safer one is from being killed [or sued] for his land." Hence, wealthy Romans were advised to distribute portions of their land to their scions, trusted allies, and the like. I call this the "Law of the Moving Target."

In the mighty Roman Empire, it was common practice for the Emperor to reward successful and loyal soldiers and political supporters with massive grants of land. In that society, as in ours 2,000 years later, there were scores of moneylenders who charged exorbitant rates of usury, went to court to win judgments against debtors, and sought to foreclose on the property of their prey.

The best advice to Roman landowners was to dilute their equity by bringing in other trusted co-owners (usually family members and close friends), so that aggressive collector-creditors and other predators would find only little left when they targeted the land.

Like his Roman counterpart, the wise contemporary debtor will seek to "shield" his property from the grasp of over-reaching creditors by diluting his percentage of ownership in the property, as by putting other people or entities on the title, and by maxing out his equity by borrowing against the equity to the limit. The practical effect of this stratagem will be to ward off creditors, because they know that a judge is far less likely to order a sale of a home to satisfy a judgment, if such a sale involves what is called "partition" of the property. If more than one person owns the property, a court would have to partition it, and then would have to play Solomon in order to resolve the mess. This, the judges do not wish to do.

Who should these co-owners be? Clearly, they should be trusted folk, family members, or longtime friends. The natural and instinctive choice is the spouse and children first. Are these wise choices?

All states have laws that enable a creditor and court to strike down "fraudulent conveyances," which are transfers of all or part of a property to another person intended to defraud creditors of their rights. It is expected that one wants to protect one's assets, but running up debts that you do not intend to pay can be considered fraud. There are certain activities that are considered so obvious that they carry what is called a presumption of fraud.

The statutes vary greatly as to what is "presumed" to be a fraudulent conveyance, but some of the factors the courts look at include the timing of the conveyance. Whether the conveyance occurred before or after the debt was declared in default, before or after the debt was incurred, or before or after the debtor was sued, all may have a bearing on how the transaction is viewed by the court. It is best to have the resources to repay one's loans. But the wise recognition that a financial calamity can happen to anyone should lead the reader to protect his assets before he gets into trouble. Attempting to hide assets after a suit has been filed is very dangerous if it is done in a way that can be viewed as fraudulent by the court.

In those Western and Southwestern states that have community property laws, a debtor is deemed to be equally liable with his or her spouse for all debts incurred by either during the lifetime of the marriage. In those states, such as California, there is little to be gained by putting a spouse on title.

But there are surprisingly few laws that strike down the transfer of property to the debtor's children, so this may be a more fool-proof option.

12

"CARJACKERS, BEWARE!"

IN THE PREVIOUS CHAPTER, we learned how to avoid being housejacked out of our own homes, but what about being carjacked by creditor-snakes and their henchman, that fabled boogeyman, the "Repo Man"?

In the 1980s, there appeared a movie called *Repo Man*, starring Harry Dean Stanton as a lowlife carjacker who was legally entitled to break into cars and repossess them on behalf of creditors.

Just as debtors fear losing their homes, they also fear losing their cars. Can a creditor take your car if you default on a loan?

If the debt does not directly concern a car loan, but something else, most states have "exemptions" codified in statutes, which allow a debtor to keep at least one car up to a certain market value. This usually is sufficient to protect the family car (unless it's a Rolls-Royce or Mercedes worth $100,000), but what about the situation where a debtor is in default on the car loan itself?

In such a situation, the lender may well dispatch the Repo Man to break into your car wherever and whenever he finds it, and seize it on sight.

THE REPO MAN COMETH AND
THEN GOETH AWAY

The Repo Man is alive and well today. He is always on call to go out and locate, seize, and tow or drive away any car on which a debtor has defaulted on his loan. Generally, based on state laws and loan documents signed by the debtor, car salesmen are legally entitled to dispatch Repo Men to seize borrowers' vehicles, even without first suing the borrowers for the amount due. Some car salesmen trot out their Repo Men when a debtor is just one or two months late in making payments, but most wait an average of five months.

After seizing the vehicle, the dealer can then sue the borrower for the full purchase price of the vehicle, and costs of towing, plus the fees of the Repo Man himself. Then the dealer can turn around and sell the very same vehicle to another buyer, and thus collect double on the very same car!

PROTECTION FROM THE
CAR SALES CONTRACT

Car sales contracts seem written in stone but, like every other contract, are subject to Moses' Law of the Law and to the Heisenberg Uncertainty Principle of the Law. The name of the game here is to avoid the Repo Man by tying up the car salesman, and his handmaiden, the car lending institution, in expensive and costly litigation before the Repo Man swings into action.

Car dealers and their financiers tend to repossess cars first and ask questions later. This is because there is a raft of penalties and fees that are triggered by the repo action, and a whole lot of sleazy operators get a payday before the situation gets back to Ground Zero. Because this is true, it is necessary to file suit against the car dealer and his financier first, before they come after you! This is necessary to obtain a pre-judgment "protective order" from the judge forbidding the dealer from repossessing the vehicle until the case is resolved (with any luck at all, that will take years).

The protective order is a necessary shield in the battle against carjackers, and is unique to car sales litigation because of the pervasive menace presented by the Repo Men. (We should add parenthetically that all of this applies equally to boat and plane sales, for the law allows Repo Men to seize those luxury vehicles as well. The law allows the Repo Men to repossess those items on the same basis as an automobile, which is to say, whenever and wherever they can be found.)

But the only real defense against the Repo Man is a legal one. Sue or countersue the dealer and manufacturer and lender for vehicle defects, fraud, breach of contract, and discrimination. Claim that these defects constitute a material breach of the contract; claim that you were defrauded when you were induced to sign the contract; and claim that you were not given enough time to read all the fine print.

One thing to be particularly aware of is that, in car repo cases, once the customer signs on the dotted line to buy the vehicle on credit, the car dealer generally disappears from the picture. You are turned over to the financing company—the bank, or hard money lender, or loan shark, or whatever. Car dealers think they can drop out of the game with impunity, but they are wrong.

The trick to fighting the Repo Man is to drag the dealer back into litigation, along with the lender and anyone else along the line who played a role in selling that lemon to you.

If you are in default or delinquent in paying the lender, it is the lender who will sue you and dispatch the Repo Man. But when you sue the lender, you are free to also sue as many other players as you can, such as the dealer, the salesman, the manager, etc. Generally, "the more, the merrier" applies here, too. We invoke Merry's Law of the Law: "The more defendants you sue, the merrier it is for you."

THE MECHANICS OF
VEHICLE DEFECT LITIGATION

Because of the nature of physics, and mechanical and physical laws, virtually every vehicle has some defects. No vehicle is perfect. Hence, there will always be some ground to claim that you were defrauded in buying the vehicle because you were not told of the defects, and that the manufacturer, dealer, and lender are guilty of material breach of contract and fraud.

With the state of manufacturing today, and the complications of computer-controlled vehicles, it is not going to be very difficult to find vehicle defects. Cars today have defective tires and computerized controls, are top-heavy and tend to flip over, have dangerous gas tanks that may explode on impact, have inadequate brakes and steering that can't always control the car in a skid, and that is just from the front page of the newspaper. But we are not just looking at the problems with your particular make and model; we are also looking at the problems of your particular car. Some have starter problems, others have engines that won't go as fast as you were told orally by the salesman, still others cannot make that curve as you were told, or they stall at odd times and you can smell gasoline in the passenger compartment. The possibilities are limitless. Because of the Law of Inevitable Defects, "Every object necessarily has some defects," no vehicle can be perfect.

Ultimately, to prove your case at trial (in the unlikely event that the case goes to trial) you will need an expert witness to testify that in his opinion, the car had "material" defects, which were not disclosed to you and that are of sufficient magnitude as to constitute a material breach of the sales contract and fraud. Expert witnesses are far more important than regular percipient witnesses in today's trial courts. Expert witnesses are generally for sale from a handbook. That is, you pay the expert to testify for you (honestly, of course), and you find his name in a Handbook of Experts, generally available for a few dollars from the local bar association or other satellite entities in your area. Then the expert goes to work, we soon have a "battle of experts," and BINGO: The case drags on ad infinitum, ad nauseum.

Apart from mechanical defects, a very fertile field for suits against the car dealer and lender concerns the clarity and fairness of the terms of the contract. Most car contracts do not properly specify exactly how much the buyer will have to pay for the car, nor what the condition and fair market value the vehicle will have at the end of the contract. Failure to disclose these tidbits of information may constitute fraud and/or breach of contract.

Other car contracts, such as leases and lease-buybacks, to name a few, contain arcane fine print that is simply incomprehensible to most laymen, and here too there is a basis for a lawsuit.

The point is to find some peg on which to hang your hat, some basis for suing/countersuing the dealer and lender, so you can save your vehicle from repossession. You can almost always find some such peg; then you can spring into action and get a protective order prohibiting repossession until the end of the suit.

Because of what is called the Principal-Agent Law, which holds that a principal is responsible for all acts of his agent, it is generally easy to sue the lender in a car defect case. The theory is that the lender is the agent of the principal (the dealer) and you sue the manufacturer on the theory that "the dealer is the agent of the manufacturer."

Once you bring the manufacturer, dealer, and lender into a lawsuit, you will trigger countersuits by them against each other, for indemnification and subrogation against one another, and you will create a "crossfire" situation in which they will pick away at each other. With each party represented by a pack of high-priced lawyer-wolves being paid $500 an hour to dream up all sorts of counterclaims they can assert against one another, you can rest assured that each party will generate a library full of complaints and countersuits. Soon, they will come around to settling the case.

Remember the logic of mathematics: It makes no sense for the merchants and their agents to spend more money on legal fees than on the total amount of money they can get from you if they only act reasonably.

Now, in car deal litigation, there is a minefield that you must take into account. Most auto financing contracts provide that if litigation results from the deal, the losing party will have to pay the attorney fees and costs of the prevailing party.

This clause is routinely inserted into contracts in order to scare the consumer out of suing and standing up for his rights. But in fact, this clause is rarely enforced and rarely invoked. Chances are, the merchant and his agents will see reason and will settle long before you have to go to trial. Trials are expensive, and cost at least $10,000 per lawyer, per side, for virtually any case, so no sane or rational merchant will spend this money to gamble on the outcome of a process that is no more predictable than a Vegas slot machine.

In short, the Repo Man is real, but he is also a scarecrow: He can be blown away by clever and astute use of the laws available to every debtor.

So, say goodbye to the Repo Man and say hello to your car!

Simon Says: "The Tenant Is Always Right"

AS THE PRICE of housing has skyrocketed in recent years, and as the economy has nose-dived, it has become harder and harder for people to own their own homes. In places like Northern California, where the median home price is about $350,000, the very term "affordable housing" has become an oxymoron. Because people increasingly can't afford to buy a house, they rent.

Accordingly, we should look at the manner in which a tenant can battle a landlord seeking to evict him or her, for failing to pay the rent, being noisy, or for no reason at all. In such cases, the tenant needs to be able to fight back in court.

Most tenants feel inherently powerless against their faceless landlords—greedy Simon Legrees—many of whom are never even seen in person, hiding behind some company name or assigning management duties to ornery building "supes." Many tenants live daily in fear of being sued and evicted if they dare to assert any complaint regarding inadequate heating, running water, or the like. They fear that the landlord will retaliate by raising the rent, suing the tenant, or other means consistent with the law of "an eye for an eye."

Although the law does favor property owners a lot, in general, this is not absolute and, like everything else in the legal arena, it can be skillfully opposed by the tenant-debtor who knows how to play the game.

Most tenants are said to be living "month to month," and are just "one month's paycheck from the street." Fear of being sued and expelled from one's apartment for failure to pay rent and then becoming homeless is a very real thing.

THE COVENANT OF HABITABILITY: THE TENANT'S BLUDGEON

First of all, if you are a tenant in a city with "rent control," such as San Francisco, you are in far better shape than most tenants, because such cities have stringent laws severely restricting landlords' rights to evict tenants.

But even without rent control, tenants do have rights and can and should assert them.

If there is something wrong with the material condition of the apartment—and there always is, because of the Law of Inevitable Defects—the tenant may be able to obviate or battle eviction by suing or countersuing the landlord. Reasons for suit can include "constructive breach of the warranty of habitability," as well as the torts of nuisance, unlawful eviction (real or constructive), breach of contract, fraud, discrimination, and other causes of action. By suing first, the tenant can seize upon state, federal, and local laws that give him the right to withhold rent until the condition is fixed to his satisfaction. In most courts, a tenant who sues first can seek a preliminary, temporary or permanent injunction from court, forbidding the landlord from evicting him while the suit drags on.

What this means is free rent for months or years, while the matter plays out in court. It is important that the tenant strike first by filing the first suit, however, for the sake of credibility.

Most people tend to believe that, "Where there's smoke, there must be fire." Therefore, they believe that if a tenant sues first, there must be something wrong with the condition of the property. Striking first gives you the upper hand, sets the posture of the case in your favor, and also tends to shield you against a lawsuit by the landlord to evict you (i.e., the unlawful detainer lawsuit).

RETALIATORY EVICTION: THE TENANT'S TRUMP CARD

Landlords are terrified of trying to evict a tenant who has first filed suit against them because it raises the specter of yet another cause of action against the landlord for "retaliatory eviction." This is a very powerful tool in the hands of a debtor-tenant facing eviction.

Having represented mostly tenants for twenty-seven years, let me assure you that I have seen the world turned upside down by aggressive and litigious tenants who have struck first and pinned the landlord against the wall with a lawsuit.

Is there something wrong with that heater? Does it not give off enough heat to warm the unit? Is there mold growing in the flat due to leaking rainwater? Does the shower or fridge fail to work properly? Is any local, county, state, or federal law regarding tenancy being violated by Wicked Simon? If so, you can grab the initiative by suing the landlord first, before he sues to evict you.

Many tenants, indoctrinated by a society that regards them as inferior for not owning real property, feel too shy or too guilty or too "stupid" to strike first. However, in a legal dispute, striking first is right. Striking first is just. Striking first is good. If you have a legitimate animus to complain about, then by all means, strike first. You will get a chance to ask questions later (during depositions and in discovery).

I have a pair of clients who have been meekly living in a ghetto slum apartment for twelve years—breathing in the mold from the leaking windows and walls, gingerly stepping around rotten floorboards, all the while paying rent and living in terror of the threat of eviction. "If we complain, we will be evicted," is their consistent mantra. So they live in a noxious miasma of fear and squalor, unable to assert their rights, forever fearful of being sued and evicted.

Many tenants in the same position believe that because they have no lease, and are living "month to month" at the landlord's discretion, they have no legal rights whatsoever and can be kicked out before the sun rises. This is not true. Even without a lease, a tenant has rights. The minute a landlord gives a tenant permission to occupy his premises, that tenant becomes a charmed "person" with "rights" in court.

I counseled my clients to forget their fears and strike first by means of a massive lawsuit against the landlord, and to refuse to pay rent until all the bad conditions were fixed.

The landlord soon brought in the mold-finding goon squads and the repairman drones and began cleaning up his act. When I asked him why he did not evict the tenants for being pests, he replied, "Then they would have sued me for retaliatory eviction."

The landlord's fears are justified: I had a client who was paying $500 a month for a slum-flat near Candlestick Park in San Francisco. She finally got the courage to withhold rent and sue the landlord, and won $400,000. I have another client who wisely videotaped her foot bouncing seesaw style on rotten wood on a deck that her Scrooge-like landlord had failed to repair. She took the landlord to court after a visitor fell through the board, and she won a cool $3 million. The landlord lost his property, as well he should have.

Personally, I have been both a tenant and a landlord, and I

can speak from the heart: If you have a problem, strike first, don't pay the rent, and ask questions later.

When you are a litigious pest, the landlord will have an extra incentive to make a settlement with you, providing that you agree to move out. I had a client who put up with a Scrooge landlord for twenty-two years. The day after we filed suit, the landlord offered her $30,000 (for starters) to move out and settle the suit.

Yes! Suing pays!

The record books are full of instant millionaires who were tenants one day, and property owners the next—following a successful suit. As with any other lawsuit, the more sympathetic the tenant is, the more likely he is to elicit a huge punitive damage award from a jury, against Wicked Landlord Simon Legree. Are you handicapped? Suffering from a debilitating disease? Old? Young with infants or small kids? Then you are a charmed plaintiff and have a good chance to hit the jackpot.

If you are disabled or handicapped, over forty years old, or a member of a protected racial or gender class, you can also sue the landlord for discrimination, and the sky is the limit for damages.

What sane landlord would risk his all on a Reno one-armed-bandit pull?

THE SAME PRINCIPLES APPLY TO COMMERCIAL TENANTS

What goes for residential tenancy also goes for commercial. A tenant with an office in a huge skyscraper may be faced with a cash flow squeeze and may be threatened with eviction, or even with a lawsuit by the landlord for the full rent due and eviction. Since commercial leases are usually much longer than residential ones, and are based on the tenant's assumption that he will have enough business to keep paying the rent for the life of his lease, commercial tenants face frequent threats of monster lawsuits from their landlords.

In such situations, where you are a tenant and cannot afford to pay the rent because your business is down or you just got robbed of your life savings by a greedy hospital or whatever, you can still play the litigation game and sue the landlord for constructive eviction. Constructive eviction is a concept that holds that if the landlord makes it impossible or difficult for you to stay in your unit, he is constructively (in effect) evicting you, and the law says you can take him to court.

Let's face it: Every office has copying and fax machines that frequently jam, do not work, and are not fixed regularly. The air conditioning and heating do not always work (especially at nights and weekends). This gives every tenant the right to withhold rent until the work is done. The mere threat of suing Simon Legree often serves to wring out a generous compromise settlement, in which Simon will sign away his rights to sue you for six figures for "breach of lease" if only you settle.

Where can tenants obtain a quick fix of their legal rights against Simon (the landlord) Legree?

There are many tenant unions in various cities that have such information for the asking. City and local rent boards provide a quick compendium of the law. In addition, that famous layman's press, Nolo Press, puts out several excellent handbooks on landlord-tenant rights and disputes.

He who seeks shall find.

Simon Legree, legendary wicked landlord of fable, is very much alive and well in the offices, apartments, and houses of every person. But remember this: Every landlord must obey Simon Legree's Law: "If the landlord is sued by the tenant for unsatisfactory property conditions, it is a mistake to seek to evict the tenant, because such efforts will generate only another lawsuit for retaliatory eviction."

Armed with Simon Legree's Law, how can any tenant lose?

PART III

DEBTORS SUE CREDITORS: DEBTORS ON THE OFFENSE

14

DISCRIMINATION: PLAYING
THE "JOKER'S WILD" CARD

AMERICAN SOCIETY HAS moved in recent years to a form of "dictatorship of the mind," a cultural censorship that permeates the entire society and ostracizes those who defy the baseline norms. This dictatorship of the mind is often expressed euphemistically as an insistence on "politically correct" speech.

The need to be "politically correct," or "PC," permeates this society's laws, workplace, and, yes, even the debtor-creditor wars (though the latter has not developed anywhere near its potential, due to lack of debtor consciousness).

The linchpin word that holds together our PC culture is "discrimination." More than any other word ever employed in America, "discrimination" is poison. To be labeled a "racist" or a "bigot" or to be accused of discriminating against anybody on the basis of their race, gender, color, creed, or physical or mental disability, is to invoke the wrath of the American PC Furies.

The classic case of PC in action is the familiar scenario in which a college professor utters a traditionally insulting word in referring to a member of a so-called "protected class." Professors are known to have been instantly discharged, blackballed, and ruined just because they used one of these appellations to describe a "protected class person" ("PCP").

In the area of credit, there are umpteen laws—federal, state, and local—that outlaw discrimination in the form of granting or denying credit, charging interest, enforcing credit contracts, collections, and the like.

The trick for the wise debtor is to pronounce himself as a "protected class person" and thereby invoke the wrath of the Furies upon any of your enemies who might even possibly be construed as practicing "discrimination."

DISCRIMINATION: THE MORAL DIMENSION OF COUNTERSUING THE CREDITOR

The law defines certain "protected classes" that include the following: anyone with a physical or mental handicap or "medical condition" or "disability;" anyone who is a "minority" by race, color, or creed (generally, racial minorities); any female (the entire female race has been declared PCP by federal, state, and local laws); anyone who is religious; and so on. To be a PCP is to elevate oneself into the lofty and rarefied air of a "protected class of person" and to entitle oneself to the full "sword and shield of the law."

Anyone who has been denied credit knows how important the "discrimination" card can be. Each denial of credit is followed by a letter with small print informing the person that if he or she feels discriminated against, he or she can file complaints with government agencies at all levels and can complain to the merchant.

That is the way it works at the start of the credit game, when you apply for credit; later on, the "D word" is rarely uttered by merchants and creditors, yet it is still there, slumbering like a giant beast waiting to be awakened.

How can one awaken the discrimination beast? Simply by

declaring oneself a member of a protected class, and then accusing creditors and collection agencies of "discriminating against me."

Discrimination is more of a broad concept than it is a concrete reality. The trick for the clever debtor is to build up a case and make it real enough to scare the oppressor-creditors into going away, and real enough to give one the right to file a lawsuit or cross-complaint or countersuit against any creditor for "discrimination."

Because of Kipling's Law ("Ink is thicker than blood"), to accuse one of discrimination in ink (e.g., in court papers filed, and/or in the media) is to turn a vague concept into a concrete reality in the minds of millions and to create a famously effective genie to grant the debtor's most ardent wish ("Make my debt go away").

We all have heard of the fabulously successful class action suits brought by PCPs alleging the "D word." A handful of black Secret Service agents filed a class action suit against Denny's Restaurant chain for racial discrimination (for seating them in a segregated "back of the room" location and denying them proper service). Before the ink was dry on the pleadings, Denny's promptly coughed up $33 million to settle the case, figuring they would lose more in customer good will if they didn't cave in. A similar case against Texaco resulted in an equally fabulous reward.

PCPs reap rewards when they are victimized by discrimination. If those black Secret Service men who sued Denny's had happened to be debtors down on their luck and pursued by a ruthless Denny's creditor-collection chain, they could have easily dissolved the debt they owed Denny's by countersuing for racial discrimination.

Discrimination is the most powerful tool in the litigious debtor's toolbox. Of course, to play the discrimination card one must be black or Hispanic or a member of some other "protected class" of minorities, must be clever, and must provide evidence of discrimination. In the Denny's case, a handful of restaurant patrons provided affidavits saying they had seen a few Denny clerks mistreat Secret Service men. That was enough for them to win the day. The Denny's restaurant chain, fearing massive customer boycotts across the nation unless they apologized and ponied up the cash, quickly fell into line and emptied its pockets into the hands of the oppressed. Texaco did likewise.

Now, what about banks and mortgage companies and the other hobgoblins of the creditor wars? Can they too be tied down on the Rack of Discrimination and stretched out until they cry "uncle"?

Why not? What is the difference between Bank of America and Denny's? The answer is "Not much," especially when looked at as legal entities that are being sued by an individual citizen.

Now, what if you are a white male under forty with no visible medical handicaps? How can you be a member of a "protected class"? Easily. The law recognizes not only conventional discrimination, but also "reverse discrimination" as a cause of action. That is, if a white male thinks he is being discriminated against because he is white and male, the law welcomes him to file suit.

He can then claim protection under the umbrella law, which holds that "It is illegal to discriminate against anyone based on his or her race, gender, age, medical condition, etc."

Because the umbrella law is a poor exercise in twisted logic, what it means, in effect, is that anybody can sue anyone for discrimination, as long as he or she frames the lawsuit artfully and pushes the right magic buttons of legal language. Not only that, but the underlying charge could actually be true. Discrimination, reverse and otherwise, *does* exist throughout our society.

We have all heard of angry white men suing big city police

and fire departments for "reverse discrimination." Many have won big-time. Today, virtually anyone can play the discrimination card against anyone else, night or day, in federal or state court, ad infinitum.

Years from now, people will probably laugh when they examine the mindless and contradictory manner in which our society (and its laws) has demonized "discrimination." But for right now, this is a fertile field for the wise debtor-litigant. A claim of discrimination—used judiciously—may lead to the reaping of great rewards.

Discrimination can be used not only as the axis of any suit against a bad creditor, but also as the "icing" on the cake of litigation. The "D word" is like a condiment, a spice that adds great pizzazz and flavor to any suit. It makes any suit "sexy," as we lawyers like to say. And we all know that sex sells.

Yes, to claim discrimination is to elevate your case into a "moral crusade," to claim the mantle of the great Martin Luther King, Jr. and other icons of our society. A claim of discrimination can transform an ordinary debtor-creditor suit into a politically correct moral cause. Such sexy attributes to a suit may well attract the interest of the "Mediacs," the news media who thrive on sensationalism, exaggeration, and Good Samaritan imagery. The Mediacs love discrimination cases. They love to stick a microphone in the face of a creditor accused of the "D word" and to play the role of Savior and Good Samaritan by glorifying the underdog and helping the "little guy" against the powerful corporate creditor behemoths.

Because the vast majority of Americans are in fact debtors, whose debt/equity ratio vastly exceeds 1.0 and continues to skyrocket with each passing day, it follows that the Mediacs' main audience consists of debtors. How many of those debtors out there in TV Land can empathize with the noble and courageous debtor who has taken on the battle against the evil discriminators in creditor boardrooms?

KING DAVID'S LAW: USING THE DEBTOR'S SLINGSHOT

Everyone knows the Biblical story of the young Hebrew shepherd boy named David, who defied great odds and slew the evil Philistine giant Goliath with a slingshot.

There is something terribly appealing about this story, because it shows how an underdog can win the day with a little pluck and luck. Because most people are in fact underdogs, and always will be underdogs, they tend to identify with David and with all the progeny of David who take on the Creditor-Goliaths in the courtroom by shouting "discrimination" and other PC buzzwords, who fight to keep their homes, their families, their children together under one roof. Every time a lawsuit is filed in this country, a gang of courtroom beat reporters takes note and looks for a sexy angle, particularly one alleging the "D word." I have filed suits and, to my amazement, have been flooded with media calls within a few hours of the filing. The hero- and drama-starved media are constantly groping for a hot and dramatic story.

Many people do not remember that the David of slingshot fame grew up to become King of the Jews and to transform himself into one of history's greatest leaders. While the evil King Saul persecuted and sought to kill him, David gathered a band of debtors and underdogs around him, and he became a leader of a new movement that ultimately culminated in his anointment as King. In the Bible, this story is described as follows: "And everyone that was in distress, and everyone that was in debt, and everyone that was discontented, gathered themselves unto him, and he became a Captain over them." (I Samuel 22:2).

David was a political, legal, and religious genius because he realized the power of the underdog to transform society. The underdogs, he knew, far outnumbered the privileged few, just as debtors in our society vastly outnumber the privileged few creditors.

King David's Law of the Law holds that "Most people will identify with the underdog and will cheer him on or join him (as in a class action or media campaign), because there are always more underdogs than overdogs."

By positioning himself as a PCP, a victim of discrimination, and an underdog armed only with a slingshot and a great heart, today's debtor warrior can strike at the heart of the enemy creditors, and can gather around him, ". . . all who are in distress, and all who are in debt . . ."

By playing the discrimination card, the clever debtor can wreak havoc among his creditor opponents. Whether as a solo litigant or as part of a class action, he can bring down the evil Philistine giant with a stone fired from his slingshot—a shot amplified 1,000-fold by manipulating the legal tools at his disposal.

15

RIDING SHOTGUN: CLASS ACTION AGAINST THE CREDITOR

IN THE LAST CHAPTER, we saw how wise David attracted followers and overthrew the evildoers in power.

In our society, King David's Law leads directly and logically into the concept of the "class action." Just as creditors shake in their boots when they hear mention of the word "discrimination," they tremble even more when they see a "class action" lawsuit sailing toward them like a battleship looming menacingly on the horizon, its 16-inch guns blazing.

What is a class action?

It is the greatest of all lawsuits, the type that brings the largest bang for the buck, and reaps a tremendous booty of damages and attorney fees. The class action is symbolized by the old Roman symbol of the Fasces, the bundle of weak individual rods made strong and unbreakable by joining ranks.

Now we turn to practical matters: How can one transform an ordinary solo lawsuit into the granddaddy of all suits, the class action? The answer is surprisingly simple. In fact, it is so simple that the surprise is that more litigants have not made use of it as a gambit in their battles with creditors.

Anyone can file any lawsuit against anyone else, and call it a "class action," simply by alleging that the individual plaintiff is representative of a class of "similarly situated" persons or entities. Different courts have different rules about verifying and defining and "certifying the class," and have convoluted rules about the need to "notify" all members of the class. Who among us has not received such an unsolicited form letter in the mail, notifying us that we are members of a class of litigants battling some evil corporate monster in some distant city or state, and offering to pay us money in the guise of "refunds" as part of the class action if we join up?

Such class action notices usually concern insurance company overcharging or fraud, banks' imposition of unconscionable and outrageous "late fees" and "overlimit fees" and the like. Indeed, there have been so many class actions out there filed against so many different types of creditors that it is virtually impossible not to find a case that is comparable to your own.

Class actions are ridiculously easy to file, but enormously expensive to defend against. The larger the creditor, the more he has to worry about, because there are more potential "class action plaintiffs" out there, and because he has a deeper pocket ripe for the plucking.

THE LEVERAGE OF LEGAL JUJITSU

To use the class action lawsuit against a large creditor is to engage in legal jujitsu, in other words, to use your opponent's own weight, size, and momentum against him. This law, which I call "Bruce Lee's Law of the Law" is a form of legalistic Kung Fu, named after the legendary but diminutive martial arts warrior and movie hero.

Bruce Lee was a genius because he realized that despite one's physically small size, a clever and resourceful person could defeat a far heavier and larger opponent. By skillful use of his arms and legs as levers that utilize the weight and momentum of the opponent, he developed and taught strategies employing jujitsu along with a fiercely determined mind.

Bruce Lee's Law of the Law can be of great help to any debtor contemplating a class action, or even a solo lawsuit or countersuit against a seemingly much more powerful creditor foe.

By setting one's mind toward the concept of defeating the creditor, and toward uniting many similarly situated, anonymous plaintiffs against creditors against whom they share a common complaint, the clever debtor-litigant can engage in legal jujitsu and use an opponent's supposed strength and weight against him.

Contrary to popular myth, a prospective litigant does not need to know the names of all of his co-plaintiffs in a class action. When you start out and are ready to file your suit in court, all you need to do is to assert that "there exists a group of similarly-situated plaintiffs" out there who are being dragged into the case unwittingly by your *tour de force* of a lawsuit. Only later—much later—will you have to come up with names and specific information on your myriad co-plaintiffs. By that time, the battleship will have left the port and will have torpedoed the creditor's vulnerable armada.

THE POWER OF APPEARANCES

The class action lawsuit employs one of Sun Tzu's famous dicta in *The Art of War*, which we will call "Sun Tzu's First Law": "In war, strategy and deception are of the utmost value . . . what counts is not what is seen, but what *appears to be seen*."

This dictum is of mighty applicability in the courtroom, as

it is in every other form of battlefield. Not only that, but it dovetails nicely with his major law, namely "Sun Tzu's Second Law," which holds that, "Most battles are won before they have even begun." We have seen that most lawsuits follow this principle and are also won before they have even begun.

The class action is the equivalent of a mighty battleship in the courtroom wars. It magnifies a litigant's power 1,000-fold, in every sense. From defense lawyers to judges, everyone dreads the class action because it consumes an enormous amount of time and resources and because defendants stand to lose millions and to reap the rewards of bad publicity.

When confronted with this venerable battleship of a suit, judges are likely to prod creditors into settling quickly before the case gets out of hand. In one stroke, the debtor will have transformed the situation from one of hopeless defense to one of invincible offense. Every cog and gear in the courtroom machinery will be turning in his favor. The pressure will be on the creditor and it will not be long before the debtor can start bringing out the champagne.

What sane creditor would want to spend $100,000 on legal fees—and reap a whirlwind of bad publicity—just to shake a debtor down for a measly $20,000 debt? The answer is simply that a rational creditor with a business to run will not do it. It just doesn't make sense. As we have seen, creditors do not squander money on enterprises with no prospect of financial gain.

16

The Last Resort: Suing the Stockbroker

FIGHTING OFF THE creditor ogre is only a part of the debtor's struggle back to financial strength. The other half of the struggle is often suing someone to regain money lost in a dubious transaction.

After all, when a tire is leaking air, even after you patch the hole you will still need to find some source of air to inflate it again.

Buying on Margin: Loss Plus Debt

Many investors buy stock "on margin." This means that they "borrow" from the broker up to 50 percent of the value of the stocks they buy. Margin accounts became so popular during the Roaring Nineties that they now account for a substantial portion of major brokers' accounts. When the stock market went up, as it did during the Clinton Boom, margin buying made a lot of sense, because it doubled an investor's power to magnify his wealth. But when the market suddenly nose-dived, as it has done under George W. Bush, the margin strategy became a

disaster, because it enabled brokers to quickly sell out their customers on short notice and without their consent, en masse.

Once you are on margin, you are in debt to the broker, and
the latter can issue "margin calls" requiring you to immediately
pony up more cash or risk being sold out without your consent
at the broker's whim, with the broker reaping huge commissions
for selling you out. This means that when the market nose-dives,
as it has under Bush's term in office, millions of investors are
sold out or forced to pour more cash into a losing venture.

Thus, many of the small investors in the boom-and-bust
market of recent years have been dual losers, both as debtor
and as market player. Many of these unfortunates have watched
the big players reap windfall profits, while they lost their shirts
as the Bush Market has turned into a bottomless pit.

LOST MONEY IS NOT REALLY LOST

So, how does the clever debtor find a way to replenish his cup
of cash?

In the past few years, since George W. Bush and the
Republicans have taken over the reins of government from
Clinton and the Democrats, we have seen a massive collapse in
the stock market. Millions of people have seen their assets disappear through major drops in the price of stocks, as well as
the collapse of the stock market's handmaidens, the IRAs,
401(k) plans, pension funds, mutual funds, retirement funds,
and everything else that was supposed to be a "nest egg" for
the innocent small investor.

At the zenith of the Clinton-era stock market success (now
dubbed a "bubble"), the Dow Jones Industrial Average rose
above 11,000. This was in early 2000, an election year.

By early 2003, the Dow had nose-dived down and stag-
nated around 8,000, and at best, the market has "moved side-
ways." Many people who had counted on their investment

portfolios to help them pay their bills have instead watched those portfolios evaporate. Those who bought stocks in such powerhouses as Enron and WorldCom have been fleeced completely: as the corporate pirate-executives have stolen the investors' money and then declared the biggest bankruptcies in world history.

The technology-ridden NASDAQ, an even more sensational stock market bubble under Clinton, has collapsed from a high of 4,000 in 2000 to a figure under 2,000 in early 2003. Most investors sought to partake of the NASDAQ rocket by investing more and more in dot-coms and other dubious high-tech stocks, and thus have felt even more pain than have the stodgy old blue chip Dow investors.

"Easy come, easy go," has been the mantra used to describe what has happened, but unfortunately for the debtor who has seen up to 90 percent of his portfolio value "disappear," this phrase is not good enough to explain "what went wrong."

The stock market has always been just a glorified gambling casino. But the Rah-Rah Nineties resembled the Roaring Twenties for many debtor-investors, because many top-notch financial institutions, brokerage firms, investment banks, and media talking heads were corrupted into making blatantly fraudulent sales pitches for bogus stocks. Those investors who deferred paying off their credit card and other debt in order to "play the market" have now found themselves holding an empty bag as well as a huge debt portfolio.

Most investors, knowing next to nothing about economics, have accepted their fate with a shrug, a nervous breakdown, a bullet to the head, a divorce, or simply a grimace. They don't realize, or even conceive of, the fact that there is life after the stock market collapse.

First of all, the money they "lost in the market" has not really been lost at all. The "Law of Conservation of Money" holds that "Money cannot be created or destroyed; it merely changes hands." At least some of the cash supposedly "lost" in the market crash has ended up in the hands of bears who sold short, or day traders who saw the trend coming and chipped at the slide all the way down. But those are only the rare buzzards who managed to pick up a few scraps. The vast majority of the investors' money wound up in the hands of scoundrels like Ken Lay, former Enron CEO and George W. Bush campaign financier, and other thieving magpies of corporate America, who stole the money in the form of higher salaries, bonuses, and outright theft.

Think about it. While Bush was raking in the cash and running the best financed campaign in history in 2000, where was his money coming from? From the likes of "Kenny Boy" Lay and his Enron cohorts. But where did they get the cash? Clearly, from foolhardy investors who were deceived by all the phony glitter that corporate America had to present, by the bogus "creative accounting" of Arthur Anderson and other "big-name" auditor chiselers, and by corporate pirates who deliberately cooked their books to make it appear that they made far more money and had far fewer debts than was the case.

Now, only the very tip of the corporate fraud scandal has been exposed by the media so far, but it is enough to give pause to the debtor seeking to recoup his lost money. When more and more suckers buy stocks in companies like Enron and WorldCom, the "market capitalization" (number of shares of stock multiplied by price per share) of such companies skyrockets, and this creates "real money, real wealth." When the corporate thieves then drain their companies of this hard cash, they are actually stealing the money of those poor debtor-investors who had been suckered into buying the stock in the first place. This is what really happened when Enron's stock collapsed overnight from $82 per share to a few pennies per share.

SUING THE BROKER: NO GUARANTEES

A cottage industry of scavenger lawyers has opened up in the wake of the stock market collapse, recruiting clients from the ranks of the Fallen Investors, promising to sue brokers en masse for giving bad and fraudulent advice to investors. In virtually every city, lawyers have taken out ads that encourage fleeced investors to sue their brokers for fraud, malpractice, negligence, and more. One such lawyer tells his clients that he can "guarantee" them that they will get their money back ("every penny of it"). He lures them in, charges them $25,000 as a nonrefundable fee, and then talks them through a boilerplate complaint form filed with the NASB (National Association of Securities Brokers) for arbitration purposes.

Now, suing your broker is okay, but what these "guarantee" lawyers fail to tell you is that any suit or arbitration is always a crapshoot, a gamble with no guarantee of success.

Moreover, because all securities brokers force their clients to sign mandatory arbitration agreements promising to refer any future dispute to the NASB for mandatory binding arbitration, you cannot sue the brokers in any court, unless you allege fraud in the inducement of the arbitration agreement. Otherwise, you are stuck in the quicksand of arbitration, which always favors the corporate defendant.

As a practical matter, the NASB follows "Kaiser's Law." This is a reference to Kaiser Permanente, the giant HMO (not the German monarch). Kaiser's Law states that arbitrators are all paid puppets of the industry, which controls the arbitration process, just as Kaiser Permanente and its cohorts control medical malpractice arbitration processes, as we discussed earlier in this book.

Following Kaiser's Law, the NASB arbitrators rule in favor of the broker in over 80 percent of all cases.

So, before you cough up a cool $25,000 on some lawyer's

vague "guarantee" of results, think twice. While Daniel survived his tour of duty in the lion's den, you are far less likely to prevail in the lion's den of the NASB.

The "scavenger pettifoggers" who promise you results are usually con artists who are careful not to "guarantee" any such results in the written contract they force you to sign. Then, after you lose your arbitration, under the Parol Evidence Rule, you can never introduce as evidence against them any oral testimony regarding what the lawyers may have told you orally before you signed, unless there is an ambiguity in the written contract.

Lawyers take advantage of the Parol Evidence Rule by promising prospective clients the moon and the stars to induce them to sign on the dotted line. While cynically changing the terms of the paper contract to state that "no representations are made as to the chances of success of the litigation claim."

For those who have lost half a million dollars or more in the recent stock market collapse and are really angry, it may not seem too bad an idea to cough up a mere $25,000 to get revenge. But you might as well kiss that money goodbye if you sign on with an "NASB" pettifogger.

While the law does state that elder citizens over age sixty-five are in a "protected class group" as far as their susceptibility to being exploited by unscrupulous stock brokers, and while stock vulture lawyers target such investors as recruits for their "lawsuits," even elderly investors generally have to meet the impossible burden of showing that they knew nothing about how the market works when the broker poured sweet poison into their ears. Who among us can seriously meet that burden?

The only way to prevail in a case against a securities broker or firm is to sue the bastards in federal or state court, claiming fraud in the inducement of the NASB mandatory arbitration agreement. In that way, you can hope to take advantage of the inexorable law of litigation economics.

But such a court suit is probably a long shot at this time. While the courts have a moral obligation to take a look at the legality of mandatory arbitration agreements in the stock market arena, it is highly unlikely that very many will seriously do so. Most federal and state judges (over 65 percent) have been appointed by pro-business Republicans, and these conservative jurists generally favor big business over the small investor.

And if the case winds up in the U.S. Supreme Court, investor-litigants will confront a court packed with Republican black robes who installed Bush in office by deciding the infamous 2000 election, and they almost always favor big business litigants.

So, suing the broker is not likely to be a very effective remedy for the fleeced small investor, but you can give the bad guys a run for the money, and some of them may settle for some percentage of your loss.

THE STEAMROLLER OF
COUNTERSUITS: ANTITRUST

THE PREVIOUS CHAPTERS have been about issues that concern the more conventional causes of action to throw against creditors, either in a suit or countersuit. Now we will discuss the granddaddy of them all, the steamroller of anti-creditor suits: antitrust violations.

Antitrust is surely one of the least understood and most arcane areas of the law. Most people have only a vague idea that antitrust laws are supposed to prevent huge companies (such as Microsoft) from monopolizing the market by unfair tactics, such as illegal "tie-in" arrangements and price-fixing. In fact, antitrust law is far more complex than this, and it involves thousands upon thousands of federal, state, and even local laws, rules, and regulations.

Antitrust law is an American invention that originated during the 1890s, when the Sherman Act was created in Congress. It continued right up to the heyday of Teddy Roosevelt and his "Trust Busting" crusade in the first decade of the twentieth century, and on into Woodrow Wilson's era. In response to the excesses of the late nineteenth-century "Robber Baron" days, when a few monopolists and oligopolists dominated many important industries, Congress enacted myriad antitrust laws that forbid one or a few large companies from dominating the marketplace in particular industries, such as railroad transportation or automobile production. The Clayton and Sherman Antitrust Acts were enacted at that time, and they still form the foundation of all antitrust laws. Since then, more obscure federal and copycat state antitrust laws such as the Lanham Act, the Robinson-Patman Act, and others have sprouted up to enable people to do battle with the corporate dragons.

Each state has enacted similar "copycat" antitrust laws, which mimic their federal counterparts but which also provide added penalties, more specific grounds, and the like.

THE POWER TO SUE FOR ANTITRUST

In many states, such as California, there is a "private attorney general" statute that allows private citizens to bring antitrust court actions against corporations in the guise of "private attorneys general" and that provides for triple damages, attorney fees, and huge penalties.

Though the antitrust laws—state and federal—are supposed to be enforced by lawsuits brought against corporate tyrants by attorneys general ("AGs"), in practice it is rare to see AGs bring such action. The exception is in egregious cases such as Microsoft, AT&T, and the like, where consumers are genuinely angry at corporate tyranny. Hence, the private statutes have been enacted in a number of progressive states.

Despite the availability of antitrust remedies, surprisingly few antitrust actions have been brought against creditors for conspiring to fix interest rates, late fees, and other terms of credit transactions. Yet there is always ample opportunity for a future anti-creditor–debtor crusader to bring such actions against the bad guys.

There is no question that creditors routinely conspire with

each other to fix interest rates, terms of credit card debt, late fees, and so on. Indeed, the whole "Visa" and "MasterCard" groups of merchants are nothing but a large "combination in restraint of trade," because they regularly trade information with each other and fix prices, interest rates, and the terms of late fees and other charges.

All you have to do as an experiment to prove this point is to apply for five or so credit cards from different merchants. You will soon see that their standards and rates and fees are virtually the same, and that the ones who turn you down or grant you a credit card will do so in amazingly similar fashion.

Antitrust law is a particularly "plastic" law in that it is really in the eye of the beholder whether particular creditors have conspired to violate the law or not. That is, what is a "price-fixing conspiracy" in one juror's or judge's mind is a perfectly legitimate exercise in "free trade" in another's.

This plasticity, combined with Newton's Laws of the Law, lends itself readily to anti-creditor suits and countersuits. What is most interesting about antitrust law is that it is extremely convoluted and expensive for creditors to defend against. This is so because when an antitrust suit is filed and a massive discovery paper war is unleashed against the creditor, the debtor-litigant has the right to demand millions of sheets of paper documents substantiating and vetting every meeting, e-mail, document, and correspondence a particular creditor ever held with any other creditors similarly situated. If the debtor-litigant is clever enough, he will turn the tables upside down and force the creditor to pay at least $100,000, if not more, in legal fees on discovery alone, and will easily bring the latter to its knees. In addition to lawyer fees, the creditor will surely have to expend a veritable fortune on expert witness fees, economist witness fees, and the like to disprove the allegations concerning antitrust violations.

Following Merry's Law, "the more defendants, the merrier it is for the debtor-litigant," it would behoove the litigant to sue

a large number of creditors similarly situated for antitrust violations. An antitrust suit is, per se, a class action because it
alleges that millions of other debtors were similarly victimized
by creditor collusion in violation of the antitrust laws.

Since most creditors and banks now operate in all fifty
states, one can theoretically drag in defendants and data and
laws from all fifty, plus the federal laws, and wreak utter havoc
on creditors scrambling to defend against such monster suits.
Each creditor who is sued will surely have to file cross-complaints for indemnification against each and every other sued
creditor, and will have to hire new counsel for those. Before
you know it, you will have created a crisscross pattern of suits
and countersuits and kicked up more dust than a twister.

Some of the most successful antitrust suits brought against
credit card giants like Bank of America and Wells Fargo have
cost these companies millions of dollars in legal fees. This
comes even though in class action antitrust suits, each individual debtor-victim-litigant suffered at most only a few dollars of
damage by being overcharged. This is due to the "Multiplier
Effect Law," which holds that one individual debtor's damages
may be relatively small, but that the total damage figures
involved become gargantuan when multiplied by millions of
other debtors similarly situated.

Even if you have suffered only damages of $1, if there are
600 million MasterCards out there, that damage figure instantly
multiplies to $600 million (not counting legal fees for the
defense), so that any sane creditor would run for cover as soon
as the bullets started flying.

ANTITRUST AND THE
CONSPIRACY TO DEFRAUD

Antitrust conspiracy can be proved fairly easily, at least as far as
a *prima facie* case is concerned. While we would ideally like to

capture a dozen bankers on videotape, sitting around an oblong table and plotting on new ways to screw the consumer over, this is not likely to happen. Most antitrust violators are far too clever and slick to be caught on tape. So it is hard to find "direct evidence" of conspiracies.

So, the law says that we can, in general, use "circumstantial evidence" to prove a conspiracy. Circumstantial evidence is entitled to just as much weight as "direct evidence" in any trial, as any standard judge's jury instruction will inform the jury.

Circumstantial evidence uses the inductive form of logic to prove a pattern from a series of "dots" that are then "connected" in court and in jurors' and judges' minds. The "dots" are like fingerprints or footprints that lead to a particular pattern, a conclusion. A classical example of such circumstantial evidence is the following: "We seek to prove that little Tommy went into the kitchen and stole cookies from the cookie jar. Nobody saw him do it, nobody filmed him doing it, but we have found footprints on the floor that match his size of foot. These footprints alone constitute 'circumstantial evidence' that he stole the cookies."

Now, it is quite possible that another person with the same size of feet as Tommy went into the kitchen, stole the cookies, and made out like a thief. But because poor Tommy lived in the house in question, and because he had a motive to steal the cookies, we can deduce that he is guilty, and we may well be able to convince a jury or judge of this fact.

Similarly, in antitrust law, we may be able to find many "footprints" that match the size of feet of Creditors A and B. We can then deduce and infer a conspiracy by connecting these dots. And that's all you have to do.

As mentioned before, because over 96 percent of all cases settle before trial, chances are that you will never have to go before a jury to prove your circumstantial case. But you need not do so because creditors know and fear you might prevail at trial, so they will probably settle. I have seen huge banks and other creditors brought down to their corporate knees by such suits, on the flimsiest of circumstantial evidence of antitrust conspiracy. With that in mind, how can you fail?

One of the major footprints linking creditors to a price-fixing conspiracy is advertising. We all know that "advertising is 90 percent of sales." When you watch various and sundry credit card companies' relentless ads on television or in the print media, notice the similarities in their pitches. When you get those unsolicited letters from credit card companies in the mail, offering you "pre-approved" credit cards and "inviting" you to "apply" for a card that is presented as virtually guaranteed, and at a certain interest rate, notice the similarities between the different companies' solicitations.

Any similarity in solicitation or advertising is *ipso facto* circumstantial evidence of a conspiracy in violation of antitrust laws. Many companies hire the same ad agencies to prepare their marketing campaigns, so it is small wonder that they can be found in violation of antitrust laws, state, federal, and otherwise.

The mere mention of the antitrust boogeyman sends shudders down the spines of even the most hardened of creditors, because they know what this means.

If you can find a lawyer or consortium of lawyers to take on an anti-creditor case in the guise of an antitrust case, you will be halfway toward reaching your goal of shaking off your creditor albatross. And if you cannot find any, you can sue on your own. As long as you appear to know what you are doing, and generate enough credibility to be heard, you will be halfway toward the goal of being debt free.

THE UNIQUENESS OF CREDIT CARDS IN ANTITRUST LAW

Credit cards are unique in many ways, as far as antitrust law is concerned. This uniqueness, duality, and ambiguity as to their operation provides fertile ground for the debtor seeking to sue the creditor.

First of all, the term "credit card" is a broad, generic term of art that encompasses many different forms of plastic. The classic credit card is a Visa or MasterCard or Discover, or the like, which is issued by a bank or other business (these days, all sorts of companies, from airlines to gasoline companies to GM and AT&T issue such cards). Such a credit card allows you to pay just a portion of the total balance each month, usually 5 to 10 percent. The broad generic term "credit card" also includes "charge cards" like American Express and department store cards (Macy's, Bloomingdale's, etc.), which may require immediate payment within a month, or which may let you pay a monthly partial percentage. While the exact terms of these cards may differ, they are basically similar in that they allow you to charge goods and services and pay back later.

Visa and MasterCard are "joint ventures." That is, they are combinations of thousands of banks and other creditor companies that share information, apply similar rules and interest rates, and market themselves as part of a singular massive entity. As such, they immediately invoke antitrust scrutiny because they involve a classic combination of different merchants pooling their heads and resources together in one common pattern of agreement or conspiracy. It is just another step to argue that they violate antitrust laws.

Yet the credit card joint ventures ("JVs") are unique in that each member maintains its own identity, at least on plastic, with unique logos and colors. They are selling the consumer-debtor an image, a corporate identity symbol, which is more a matter of style and illusion than of substance.

There are a total of about 700 million Visa cards out there, and 500 million MasterCards, though the actual number of issuers ranks in the hundreds of thousands. In fact, any company can buy into the Visa and MasterCard system and issue its own credit card with its own logo, providing that it adheres to the general rules and regulations of the parent JV. This sounds like a textbook case of antitrust conspiracy, doesn't it?

Econometric studies by reputable economists have found a shocking lack of real competition between credit card issuers, and an even more shocking conspiracy to fix prices and terms. This sort of readily available economic study can be used as "evidence" in your antitrust lawsuit against the bad guys, and you don't even have to pay for it! You can ask the court to "take judicial notice" of such studies, and bingo! You have the bad guys right where you want them.

One such celebrated study, by Laurence Ausubel in the *American Economic Review* in 1989, concluded that the credit card industry was a "paradox" in that "credit card interest rates were virtually constant for a decade (from 1982 to 1989), ranging between 17.8 and 18.9 percent, and that banks made three to five times as much profit on their credit card lending as they did overall."

Ten years after the study, the average credit card interest rate was still found to be hovering at about 16 percent. The same is true in 2002, and this despite the fact that the federal prime rate and mortgage rates have been cut to their lowest levels in forty years, well below 5 percent. This startling fact suggests that credit card issuers have conspired to fix their interest rates and have kept them usuriously high despite a massive cut in their own cost of capital.

Why are credit card (CC) rates so high? Issuers like to justify their fleecing of the consumer by claiming that "credit cards pose a very high risk of default."

While it is true that CCs are unsecured and that the rate of default increases as the economy tanks, this explanation rings hollow. The real answer is greed.

AUXILIARY SERVICES AS A BASIS FOR
SUITS AGAINST CREDITORS

Credit card issuers can differ widely in "auxiliary services" they offer their members. These days, many of them offer debtors "bonus points" and "frequent flyer miles" and the like, which can theoretically be redeemed at a later date for free services, free flights, "credit," and so on. Yet each of these deals, intended as bait to suck in the consumer, can be challenged and attacked in an antitrust and fraud lawsuit against the issuer on the basis that the bait involved fraudulent or misleading facts or promises.

Did you really understand what the issuer meant when he said that he would "guarantee" you a free flight to Europe if you accumulated 20,000 points? Were those points really explained to you? Were you literally told what you had to buy in order to qualify, and what type of room you would get?

In addition to offering you points and free trips and extra miles themselves, credit card issuers also often affiliate themselves with specific merchants, particularly in the travel industry, and offer bait-and-switch deals that look great on paper but that conceal important details. A typical example is the major hotel chains that promise you rooms for free if you have accumulated enough points on your Visa or MasterCard or Amex card. What they do not tell you clearly, however, is that such rooms are limited to very minimal "availability," a vague term which often renders the promise meaningless.

I once tried to redeem credit card points at a large hotel chain for a hotel room in Berlin. I was told that all rooms were booked for the next six months at all hotels in the chain in Berlin. Only a limited number of rooms were held for the credit card redeemers, and I had to sue to find out what percentage of rooms were so held: generally below 3 percent.

Because so many merchants, issuers, and chains were part of this conspiracy, I sued for antitrust violation as well as fraud and breach of contract, and in that way I got out of paying a huge credit card bill.

The chains always deceive the debtor in some way. They imply that their free rooms and flights are readily available, at least 90 percent available, but in fact they have very few rooms available, and you will be lucky if you can reserve such a room years before vacation time.

THE "LOWER INTEREST RATE" FRAUD

Other credit card companies offer auxiliary services, such as "lower interest rates," if you "transfer your balance" from one credit card to another.

What they fail to tell you is that the new "lower" interest rate will not affect the original usury you owe the original creditor, and that there is a time limit (typically a few months, almost always less than a year) during which they "guarantee" lower rates.

The average interest rate on a credit card is about 16.7 percent. The companies who promise you lower rates generally limit those rates to a few months, then overcompensate by charging you 22 percent the next year.

Is that what you really signed up for?

If not, SUE SUE SUE!

Another major issue that the bad guys never tell the debtor about is when and if they can revoke your credit card or reduce your "credit limit," even if you have paid your bills on time for decades.

This issue is a major ground for litigation, because credit card companies frequently play games with even the most solid debtor by arbitrarily canceling his credit card or reducing his credit limit for ambiguous reasons. Such as a deterioration of his FICO credit rating.

Credit card issuers "move in mysterious ways," all right. They follow their own rather dubious and arbitrary "credit risk profiling" computer models (typically sold to them by ambitious and equally deceptive merchants for a quick buck). Perhaps your credit "FICO" score has been lowered by anonymous bureaucrats somewhere out there, perhaps by mistake because of a false negative report by one merchant. These models and credit scores tell creditors that for some reason or other (and usually no rational reason), you are a bigger credit risk than you were when you first got your credit card. So they send you a computer-generated small-type letter in the mail one fine day, informing you that your card has been canceled or that your credit limit has been decreased. Some are even so sinister as to keep decreasing your credit limit monthly, or bimonthly, until there is no limit left, even while you pay them on time, and they then axe you altogether.

The question is, "Do you still have to pay your credit card bills if you have been truncated this way?"

I call this the "Truncator's Law of the Law," for it holds that a creditor can "truncate" any debtor at any time, by reducing his credit limit arbitrarily—and many of them do this regularly—and the debtor has a right to withhold payment on the entire amount due, and to SUE SUE SUE.

If you are truncated by a creditor, as many of my clients are, my advice to you is to stop paying your bill and send the lender a strong letter informing him that by truncating you, he has materially breached his contract with you, defrauded you, damaged your credit, and violated the antitrust laws. Antitrust comes into play because most creditors "share" similar "debt risk computer model" data provided to them by those twenty-two-year-old Einsteins of dot-com fame, who generate the computer models and sell them to the creditors. Because all those thousands of conspirators who belong to Visa or MasterCard and other credit cards share this data, you have a basis to allege antitrust violation (as well as fraud and breach of contract), and so you can bring the bad guys down.

18

"THEY MADE ME DO IT": PLASTIC UNLIMITED AND THE DUTY TO WARN

ONE OF THE CAUSES of action a debtor may consider filing against his creditor as a means of disputing a debt is based on our society's increasing obsession with "victimhood."

America, once the land of the free and the home of the brave, has largely become the land of the oppressed and the home of the victim.

We have all heard the infamous joke about the unhappy teenager who sued his parents for "wrongful life" for giving birth to him. Now we have the endless parade of unhappy "victims" who see themselves as set upon by forces beyond their control. They are victimized by bad employers firing them at will; by bad drivers "intentionally or negligently" hitting them on the street; and by a big, bad government wolf that devours them with high taxes and poor services.

This fact, that Americans cannot accept the role of blind chance in human life and must always find someone to blame for their woes, may seem to be a simple joke, but it offers a powerful weapon to the determined debtor. After all, juries are

largely made up of people who see themselves as victims, so
they may prove fertile ground for anti-creditor lawsuits, if the
case is spun in the right way to them.

THE FRAUD OF CREDIT ADDICTION

People in this country suffer from a virtual pandemic of con-
sumerism. This has created a culture of people buying on credit
beyond what they can afford. Such spending is actually lauded
by creditors and politicians as spurring the economy and creating jobs.

On top of this, there are studies in the medical field that
conclude that manic-depressives in a manic phase will go on
spending sprees in order to get "high." It is part of their sickness
that this euphoric excess energy will find an outlet in unre-
stricted spending. If such people have been given credit cards
to spend money that they don't have, they will be sure to do it.

The fact is that creditors exploit consumers' innate psychological weaknesses of all kinds. Those with problems of vulnerable egos, and those who suffer from boredom, depression, or
manic episodes, will divert those problems into irrational and
unjustified spending. The credit card companies and those who
profit from promoting the creditcard industry prey upon those
weaknesses to con individuals into signing up for plastic and
then buying things they don't need on credit, relentlessly.
Rather than responsibly restricting those for whom plastic is a
dangerous source of addiction, these peddlers of plastic shame-
lessly promote the so-called benefits of credit and promote the
illusion that their customers are getting something for free.

Studies show that many people who charge a purchase
"subconsciously" believe that the credit company will somehow
make a mistake and not put the charge on their bills. In fact,
erroneous noncharges are rare; far more common are bogus
charges put on a monthly statement "by error" or by deliberate

fraud. Credit companies and banks often hire unskilled, lowly paid clerks who process credit card information, steal the credit card numbers, and sell them to bandits in the black market. These bandits have sophisticated machines that can duplicate a credit card from such inside information.

When the consumer notices a bogus charge on his monthly statement—*if* he notices it—chances are he will not bother to challenge it. Up to 20 percent of all erroneous charges are paid blindly by the consumers.

Even when the consumer does in fact charge goods on his card, the question is, to what extent should the creditor be held responsible for deceiving the consumer into buying things on credit that he or she does not really need? Does the creditor have any kind of "duty" to the consumer to "warn" him of the dangers of excessive credit use, just as cigarette manufacturers have a duty to warn smokers of cancer? For many people, credit use is an addictive sickness in much the same way as uncontrolled gambling is. It is shameful that a gambling casino will let a person who is showing addictive tendencies—and who is not really in control of himself—gamble until he is destitute and his family and children are made destitute by his illness. Yet credit card companies will do the same thing with someone who has a weakness for spending relentlessly. Yet within the law there is an equal and opposite tendency to make a perpetrator who preys on the weaknesses of a victim responsible for the harm that the victim suffers as a result. This doctrine does fit in with the theory of fraud. If someone knows that someone else is susceptible to a misrepresentation and then uses that knowledge to take the person's money, he has basically defrauded that person.

This area of the law is based on the "Eggshell Law of the Law," which holds that "a wrongdoer takes a victim as he finds him: with an eggshell head or a head of lead."

The Eggshell Law, one of the most important laws of the law

you will ever encounter, is honored in every court, state or federal. It maintains that even if the creditor did not know the consumer had an eggshell mentality, the former is guilty of inducing the latter to harm himself by overspending beyond his means.

Plastic credit cards are like illegal narcotics or nicotine in cigarettes. They are bad for the consumer. They create and then profit from an "irresistible impulse" to buy everything in sight on impulse. In essence, they are addictive.

How do credit cards differ from dope or nicotine, if at all? As Hamlet might say, "That is the question."

THE GROWTH OF VICTIMOLOGY

Our society has been moving toward a "pan-victimization mentality" for at least the past twenty years. Whenever something untoward happens to someone, our tendency in this society is to blame someone else and to sue or arrest that person.

More and more, the psychology and ideology of victimology has become ingrained in our culture: If there is a flood and people get killed, it must be someone else's fault; if we are in an accident of any kind, it must be someone's fault.

This pervasive victimology can find its way straight into the courtroom. That is, when we overspend on credit, we can allege that the merchant-creditor breached a duty to us to save us from ourselves, just as we allege now in court (often successfully) that cigarette companies breached a duty to smokers to prevent them from harming themselves.

What is the difference between a smoking junkie who has smoked cigarettes for thirty years and a consumer who has used plastic for thirty years?

This concept, of a Super-Duty owed by merchant to consumer to warn the latter of the dangers of plastic addiction, has been evolving as a theory of common law in general as our society has turned more and more toward victimhood as a national philosophy of life. It has even been codified, as in the laws requiring certain companies to post all kinds of "warning" signs on their goods and services.

The clever debtor-litigant, following the "Cook's Law," which holds that as litigants we are "cooks" seeking to add as much spice and condiment to the stew as we can, will assert this as a theory of "negligence" against his creditor foe. He will assert: (a) that the creditor has a duty to warn him against excessive use of plastic to live above his means; and (b) that the creditor breached that duty by failing to so warn the credit card junkie.

This is a classical two-punch *prima facie* case of "negligence," and it can work in creditor-busting too.

Creditors do not, as a rule, post "warnings" about the dangers of excessive plastic use. They do not obtain "true informed consent" of the user because they do not warn the user of how long it will take him to pay off $10,000 in debt at 20 percent annual interest rate (forty years). Nor does the creditor warn of the consequences to the consumer's life and credit record if he cannot pay his bills. Rather, the creditors assume the consumer knows all this stuff, and they hoist their warning, *Caveat emptor*—Buyer beware.

But that's just not good enough any more in our victim-hood-based society.

The creditor's duty to warn is especially acute vis-à-vis teenagers, college students, and other "eggshell-head consumers" who just don't have the seasoned judgment to realize what they're getting themselves into by signing onto "Plastic Unlimited." They are not told of the dangers of plastic addiction or of the actual ultimate cost, in interest and years, of charging some goods or services on plastic.

I say that all consumers should be told of these dangers, and that lack of full disclosure constitutes a form of fraud-by-concealment.

19

FIGHTING COLLECTION
AGENCIES WITH THE LAW

WHEN THE ADDICTED consumer is down and out, KO'd by too much plastic, he is prey to all sorts of parasites in the credit industry's collection game.

Not only credit card issuers themselves, but also their nefarious offspring—the collection agency pit bulls—pounce upon any prostrate consumer with a vengeance.

Because of the notorious excesses of the collection industry, each state, as well as the federal government, now has a Fair Debt Collection Practices Act, or FDCPA, on the statute books. In almost all cases, the state laws are modeled on the federal template. These laws are designed to protect debtors from unscrupulous and heavy-handed debt collection practices by creditors and collection agencies. Since debt collection practices are very often vicious and unethical, these laws can come in very handy. Yet they are but one arrow in the debtor-litigant's arsenal of weapons against the creditor.

To see how this act works, let's examine the federal statute in detail. The federal FDCPA is to be found in the federal code, title 15 U.S. Code section 1692. This statute was enacted by

Congress in 1977, in the heyday of the "consumer rights" movement spearheaded by Ralph Nader and his Nader's Raiders and a host of "consumer-oriented" politicos.

Section 802a of the federal FDPCA states in a glowing preamble:

"There is abundant evidence of the use of abusive, deceptive and unfair debt collection practices by many debt collectors. Abusive debt collection practices contribute to the number of personal bankruptcies, to marital instability, to the loss of jobs, and to invasions of individual privacy."

Yes, this still is the law, though it sounds as if it should have vanished along with the myriad other consumer protection acts swept away by the Reagan-Bush anti-consumer steamroller that has dominated politics in this country for most of the past two decades.

So what does all this mean? Section 805a is the key portion of the FDCPA. It says that without a court order or permission of the debtor, a debt collector ("DC") may not communicate with a consumer regarding collection of a debt: (1) at any "unusual" time or place inconvenient to the debtor (normally, any time outside of 8 A.M. to 9 P.M.); and (2) if the DC knows that the debtor is represented by a lawyer regarding the debt, the DC cannot contact the debtor directly.

Section 805a also says that a debt collector cannot contact the debtor at his place of employment if the DC is aware that the employer prohibits the debtor from receiving such debt collection messages there.

Section 805a is something of a joke in today's world, because DCs violate it regularly and with impunity. Tell them you have a lawyer, give them his address and phone, and they will ignore you and still call you at any time they want. Their attitude is, in general, "Sue us if you dare."

Nonetheless, the law is still on the books and can be used

to sue the DC and creditor "if you dare." As we shall see, there is plenty of reason to take that dare.

Section 805c adds the following rule: If a debtor notifies the DC in writing that he refuses to pay the debt or that he wishes the DC to cease further communication with him, the DC shall not communicate further with the debtor, except: (a) to advise the debtor that all further debt collection efforts are being terminated; (b) to notify the debtor that the DC may invoke certain remedies that are ordinarily invoked by DCs, such as suing the debtor; or (c) where applicable, to notify the debtor that the DC or creditor intends to invoke a specified remedy.

Section 805d adds, parenthetically, that the term "consumer" in the statute includes the debtor's parents, spouse, guardian, executor, or administrator.

Section 807 of the law outlaws "false, misleading, or unfair practices" by the DC. These dirty tricks, which are outlawed, include allegations by the DC that he is somehow affiliated with the U.S. government. The law also forbids DCs from making any false representations as to the "character, amount, or status of any debt," or any services or pay the DC may get for his efforts. It also prohibits the DC from making any false allegations that the DC is a lawyer, any threats that failure to pay the debt may result in imprisonment of the debtor or seizure, garnishment or seizure or sale or attachment of any property or wages of the debtor, etc. Failure by the DC to observe this law may be punishable by fines (good luck in convincing the government to impose such fines), and can make the DC and creditor susceptible to a lawsuit by the debtor for monetary damages in federal court for such violations of the law.

Finally, section 808 of the law states that the DC may not use any "unconscionable or unfair means" to collect a debt. The term "unconscionable or unfair" is vague and can mean anything (thus providing fertile soil for a lawsuit by the debtor against the DC-creditor); though the act does give some examples, these are not meant to be all-inclusive. These include: (a) soliciting a postdated check for the purpose of using it as a pretext to bring criminal action against the debtor; and (b) threatening to take "extra-judicial action" to seize the debtor's property. Samples of extra-judicial action might include breaking his legs, stalking him, harassing his friends and relatives, and so on.

Sections 804 and 805 of the act prohibits DCs from contacting any third persons about your debt.

YOUR REMEDIES IF YOU SUE UNDER THE FDCPA

Section 813 of the FDCPA gives you a statutory basis to sue a DC in federal court within one year of the occurrence for actual damages, attorney fees, and punitive damages for violating the law.

Each state has a copycat FDCPA of its own, which sometimes go beyond the federal statute in specifying other types of "unfair or unconscionable" debt collection practices proscribed by the law. You can sue DCs and their creditor principals and agents under those state laws in state court in separate suits, or you can sue them in federal court as part of your federal FDCPA suit. In the case of the latter, the state causes of action are called "supplemental jurisdiction."

You are better off suing the DC-creditors in both federal and state court, following Merry's Law, "the more the merrier." If you have the time, determination, and strength of character to go after them in both courts, you will double their defense costs and also double your chances of winning (buying two lottery tickets gives you twice as good a chance of winning as does one).

If you sue an out-of-state DC-creditor in a state court, he may seek to "remove" the action to federal court, under what is known as "diversity jurisdiction." This maintains that if all defendants hail from a different state than all plaintiffs, any case can be removed from any state court to a federal court.

This diversity law is a remnant of the Horse and Buggy Days when it was thought that federal courts were generally "more fair" to nonresidents than were state courts. Today, the rule is absurd and should be repealed. Juries in federal and state courts are likely to be virtually identical, and our world is so global that it hardly makes any difference if the defendant is an out-of-state company or a local yokel.

But don't expect the diversity law to be repealed any time soon. The law favors well-heeled creditors and DCs, and they show no hesitation in invoking diversity jurisdiction to get into federal court.

The only real way to defeat diversity jurisdiction removals, or to at least head them off at the pass, is to have at least one defendant from the same state as at least one plaintiff. If you can accomplish that bit of bookkeeping in your lawsuit, then you will make it impossible for all defendants to hail from different states than all plaintiffs.

If you sue a company and do not know which state is its domicile, you can easily find that out by looking it up on the Internet or phoning the company headquarters and asking the legal department or the CEO's office where the company is domiciled. Many large companies are headquartered in Delaware, even if they have only a token presence there. Delaware is favored because its corporate taxes are lower than many other states, or at least the taxes were lower when the company was formed.

In short, the FDCPA affords one a great opportunity to sue the creditor or his minion, the DC, and to countersue them. All you have to allege is that they violated the law by engaging in "unfair and unconscionable" debt collection practices, whatever that means.

20

AIM HIGH:
AIM FOR SETTLEMENT

THROUGHOUT THIS BOOK, we have spoken in general terms about the ultimate goal in any debtor-creditor conflict: to *settle* the dispute on terms favorable to you, the debtor.

What you really want out of a case is ultimately something that you as the debtor can live with: some reduction in the amount of debt, or a reasonable repayment schedule. The most desirable result, of course, would be total cancellation of the debt.

DETERMINING A REALISTIC OUTCOME:
WHAT DO YOU WANT?

While cancellation of the debt is your ultimate goal, it is often not the most reachable or the most reasonable goal within your grasp. To win a complete cancellation of your debt, it depends on how much is owed, how strong your counterclaim is against the creditor and his agents, and other intangibles. In general, the smaller the total debt, the easier it is to win cancellation; the larger the debt, the tougher it is to get off scot-free. Somewhere in between lies a reasonable range of settlement that might be called, "within the ballpark."

But even within that range of reasonableness there is an unavoidable element of unreasonableness. Engaging in settlement negotiations is an art in itself. The first thing to realize is that *all settlements are arbitrary*. It cannot be emphasized too much that there is no absolute formula, or key, upon which you can frame your settlement. Negotiating is a process, and an element of unpredictability is always an inherent part of the process. I call this the "Law of Entropy of the Law": "All settlements are arbitrary."

The concept of entropy, in physics, means randomness, chaos, and lack of rules. It is axiomatic, both in physics and in the law, that the amount of entropy is always increasing.

Every time a case is settled, because the settlement is ultimately arbitrary and chaotic, the total amount of entropy in the legal world increases, by the degree of the settlement.

During twenty-seven years in the practice of the law, this author has seen over and over again scenarios in which the very same set of facts, in two virtually identical cases, have led to wildly different settlement outcomes. Let's just take a couple of examples. In one case, Debtor A owed Bank Z $10,000 in Visa card debts. Debtor A defaulted on his debt and was sued. Debtor A countersued for fraud and breach of contract, and discrimination, and settled the case for $2,000 as payment in full. The effect was that $8,000 of debt was wiped out and sent to the Entropy Mill.

In another case, virtually identical to the first, debtor B owed $10,000 to Bank X on a MasterCard debt. He too countersued the Bank for fraud, breach of contract, and discrimination. He settled for $7,000, and thus only $3,000 was sent to the Entropy Mills.

What was the difference between A and B?

Part of the difference lay in the very concept of entropy, randomness, and chaos. Debtor B was less effective and had more fragile nerves than Debtor A. Debtor A negotiated against a "nicer" representative of Bank Z than did Debtor B with Bank X.

But ultimately, the very same set of facts produced two very different outcomes, based on (a) chance (including the skills and hard-nosed nature of the bank representative); and (b) the relative negotiating skills of each player in this game.

Realizing the overwhelming applicability of the Entropy Law of the Law, we can nonetheless identify certain negotiating techniques that every debtor can use to bring about the best possible settlement under the conditions.

NEGOTIATING FOR SETTLEMENT: THE RULE OF THREE

The first rule of negotiating is "Aim low." No matter what you think the case dispute is worth, no matter what you think is a "fair" or "reasonable" settlement of the case, you must always, always, always aim at least three times lower than the amount you are willing to accept.

For example, if someone owes Wells Fargo Bank $10,000, and that person is prepared to pay $2,100 to settle the case, it is recommended that a proper place to begin the negotiations is to offer to settle for one-third (at most) of that amount, $700.

Aiming at least three times lower than the amount you are willing to settle for gives you a realistic range of negotiations, does not cost you credibility, and prevents "free falls" and any breakdown in negotiations. It will also send to the opponent a clear signal that there is a willingness to be reasonable if only he will be reasonable.

IN NEGOTIATION, STAYING POWER IS THE KEY

The second rule is the "Wine Aging Law of the Law": "A lawsuit, just like a fine wine, gets better as it ages." In the case of wine, despite having the very same molecules and liquid from start to finish, in fact it has an entirely different taste and aroma. So too a settlement offer can get better with time as it ages. Even if the bank turns down your $700 offer to settle at the start of the case, it may soon change its position as the case ages, as its legal bills and uncertainties of litigation weigh in, and as it begins to experience litigation fatigue.

This rule works as long as the debtor possesses a good chunk of staying power, which provides the ability to continue stalling on the case until a good settlement comes along. With that power, a litigant can usually outlast the creditor because the latter is in the position of having to pay out far more money in legal fees than the game is worth.

I have never ceased to be amazed by the sheer volume of cases that started out with a creditor offering "nothing" to settle a debt, and seeing that very same creditor turn around eight or twelve months later and say, "It's just not worth it." The Wine Aging Law works.

WAIT OUT THE OTHER SIDE

The third basic rule of settlement negotiations is, "Don't blink first." I call this the "George Washington Law," which is taken from General Washington's famous orders to his outnumbered colonial troops as they faced the Redcoats during the Revolutionary War: "Don't blink first."

Washington was a superb negotiator as well as military commander and statesman. He succeeded in "negotiating" a settlement to the War of Independence because: (a) he did not blink first; (b) he waged his battles and chose the venues carefully, thus draining the enemy of blood and money over years; and (c) he started out demanding far more than he was ultimately ready to settle for.

The British did not "lose" the Revolutionary War. They "settled" it by giving up and settling for certain conditions, including granting the Colonies their independence, and receiving in turn from Washington promises that British loyalists would be treated mildly after hostilities ceased, promises regarding future trading between the mother country and the colonies, and other face-saving terms. The British could have gone on fighting for years, because they had vastly superior trained manpower and artillery as well as the wealth to crush the colonial rebels. But they soon realized how much this would cost them and they "blinked first."

Mohandas "Mahatma" Gandhi, a major anticolonial leader in India, realized the value of the art of negotiation. He staged a campaign of sustained nonviolent resistance until the British gave up and came to a settlement: In 1947, the Redcoats agreed to go home in exchange for some economic and political promises from the Indians.

In the United States, Martin Luther King Jr., adopted Gandhi's nonviolent tactics wholesale. King and his followers staged countless sit-ins and other forms of nonviolent protest until laws were enacted and enforced to eliminate segregation, discrimination, and a host of other evils.

In each of these historical examples, a vastly outnumbered underdog won the day by sustained commitment to the struggle, and by skillful negotiation and settlement of the dispute. While these conflicts involved nominally political issues, the political issues were often the result of relative creditor and debtor relationships. It has often been said that the American Revolution was "really fought over the price of tea and taxation without representation." What really angered American colonials was the fact that they were in debt to the British. Similarly, Indians and other colonial peoples were debtors vis-à-vis their imperial lords, the Redcoats, and they finally decided that they had had enough.

The economic theory of history is, of course, riddled with contradictions and exceptions, because there is a major role for chance and randomness and entropy to determine the outcome of struggles, but the key role of successful negotiating strategies must be given its rightful credit.

THE CREDITOR WANTS SETTLEMENT MORE THAN THE DEBTOR DOES

What is interesting about analyzing these historical examples, however, is the fact that the Redcoats always gave up because: (1) they didn't think the cost was worth keeping up the struggle; and (2) they thought they had other, better things to do with their time and resources.

Similarly, any major creditor in a debt dispute can and will realize that he cannot sustain an indefinite legal war of attrition costing him massive legal fees. He will realize soon that his time and resources would be better spent by chasing other things, such as other debtors who are "bigger fish to fry." This is called the "opportunity cost" of perpetual litigation.

Wells Fargo and Bank of America really don't care about individual debtors, who are mere statistics, digits, to them. Rather, they care about running a smooth and efficient debt-collection assembly line. If one "machine-debtor" in this assembly line keeps breaking down and costing the bank money, the bank would much sooner cut its losses than stay in a sustained campaign lasting many months or years with an uncertain outcome.

Why would Bank of America want to spend $20,000 in legal fees in order to chase down one recalcitrant debtor for $500? It could far more easily use its muscle and bullying tactics to shake down twenty other debtors in the same amount of time, and with far fewer resources to expend. "It just isn't worth it, it just doesn't pay" is a conclusion the challenged creditor will soon reach.

PART IV

HOW COURTS WORK: THE BLACK ROBES AND OTHER PLAYERS IN ACTION

21

MASQUERADE AT THE HOUSE OF JUDGES

EVERY LAWSUIT IS like a living, protean organism. It lives in a big house: the courthouse. It has a beginning, a middle, and an end, and it changes like a chameleon as it progresses. It is not fixed in stone, and component theories of action can be changed to conform to the evidence uncovered during discovery. This is known as "relating back to amend the complaint to conform to the evidence." Each case possesses fluidity.

Most court rules allow you to plead inconsistent and contradictory legal theories, so long as you write them in a coherent and comprehensible manner. Under rules of "Notice Pleading," upheld in every court, due process merely requires that the defendant (or cross-defendant) be given reasonable notice of what you are suing him for.

The Grand Monitors of the court system are those fabled beings in black robes, the Judges. These are the egoists who want to be addressed only as "Your Honor" (though you may feel that many, if not most, deserve to be addressed as "Your Dishonor"), and who preside over the progress of the case.

When you first file your suit or countersuit in the courthouse, you will initially encounter an army of faceless clerks, most of whom think they are smarter than lawyers and who like to help the "Pro Pers"—that is to say, the people who represent themselves *In Propria Persona*. These clerks enjoy tweaking the noses of the stiff-shirted lawyers ("suits") who disdainfully look down on them, and they are actually nicer to the Pro Pers. So if you are not a lawyer, you are already ahead of the game when confronting the "doormen" of the court system, the clerks.

Often, clerks and their supervisors are useful sources of information, and I have found that they often know more about a technical issue or rule than do the judges and lawyers themselves.

But once your case is "born" and given a number, you will sooner or later encounter that dreaded Beast of the Abyss, the Judge.

COURTROOMS: THE KAFKAESQUE DRAMA

In Franz Kafka's short story *Before the Law*, there is an excellent caricature of a typical judge, who masquerades as a gigantic, fierce, red-bearded doorman. A nameless man from the country comes to the court seeking to enforce his rights, and is stopped at the entrance gate by this terrifying figure. This doorman warns him that he cannot gain entry into the House of the Law until "the word" comes down, and that there are many other doormen even more fearsome than him inside. The man begs for admission and is denied. He stays there for years, hoping to plead his cause, growing old and decrepit and discouraged. Finally, he gives up the ghost without ever receiving an explanation of why he has not been given a chance to plead his cause.

With a few minor changes, this is an accurate description of many courthouses and judges in real life. In twenty-seven years before the bench, this author has found only a handful of judges worthy of respect, people actually dedicated to the "concept" of justice, men and women of integrity who actually read the briefs and papers filed, and who try to play Solomon when it is time to decide a case.

As for all the others, Kafka had it right in describing their mentality: mindless bureaucrats.

Recently, a retired California Supreme Court judge told me something that should be emblazoned in every courtroom in the country: "Courts are not about 'Justice.' Courts are about having someone make a decision when two sides can't decide the dispute for themselves."

That brilliantly lucid and honest statement—rare for a "black robe" in any setting—speaks volumes. As the eminent jurist has requested anonymity, I call this "Judge Grumpy's Law of the Law."

Today, in any courtroom in this country, there is a vast masquerade going on as armies of black-robed men and women are pretending to be "fair and neutral" arbiters, while in fact they are little more than glorified administrative clerks, cogs in an incredibly inefficient machine that does not work. Their main goal is to clear their calendars of cases. They are, in the final analysis, in the disposal business.

Because of the massive increase in the number of lawsuits filed in this country (it is estimated that there will be about 35 million civil suits filed in 2003, one for every ten people in the country), the courts have simply been unable to handle this flow of gobbledygook. This is due not only to the massive avalanche of lawsuits flooding the courts, but also to courts' notoriously inefficient administration of what they call "justice." Courts, often run by judges who like to keep "bankers' hours" and who are far more interested in stroking their own egos than in dispensing justice, are simply too archaic, inconsistent, and stodgy to be able to handle the modern flow of cases in assembly-line fashion. In addition, judges are notoriously underpaid, with the average American judge earning far less money ($100,000) annually than the average law school *graduate,* and judges thus have little motivation to improve their courthouse dinosaurs. Even federal judges, supposedly the *crème de la crème* of American jurists, earn only $150,000 per year, while your typical newly minted staff lawyer earns an average of $170,000 just out of law school.

The United States has 40 percent of all the world's lawyers, there is a law school on almost every corner, and almost anyone seeking to find a lawyer to work on "contingency" can easily find one. In a typical contingency fee agreement, all legal services performed by the lawyer are gratis unless money is recovered from a defendant, in which case the lawyer gets between 33 and 50 percent of the hit.

Thus, standing against a small cadre of underpaid and inefficient black robes at the courthouse, there stands a huge army of trial lawyers and plaintiffs out there ready to pounce, like the 10,000 Indians who annihilated Custer at the Little Big Horn.

THE SETTLEMENT MACHINE: THE PLAINTIFF'S SECRET WEAPON

Faced with such a mass avalanche of lawsuits and lawyers, the black robes' closely guarded secret is that they have given up trying to administer "Justice" at this Little Big Horn of courthouse battlefields, and have become little more than "Settlement Machines."

We all know of the few famous Supreme Court judges, like the right-wing ideologues Scalia and Rehnquist, who become mini-celebrities. But the vast majority of judges in this country are in fact the diametric opposite. Most judges in the country are mediocre political appointees, who toil (if you can call it that) in anonymity and who live obscure lives of masquerade in which they keep the "bankers' hours" of legend that not even bankers have any longer. They take as many holidays and days off as possible, go home early, and do little more than process endless lawsuits toward the finish line of "settlement."

The U.S. court systems lags eons behind the rest of the world in terms of technological efficiency. Most courts still process claims by hand, instead of by computer, and "electronic filing" is a rarity, an "experimental" program in very few court-rooms across the country.

Because of their arrogance, mediocrity, and pomposity, most judges do not realize that they have been reduced to glorified clerks, and they stubbornly cling to their petty fiefdoms with arcane, hideously inefficient "fingerprints" and rules that do little more than glorify their own petty egos.

In California's fifty-eight counties, every county courthouse has a different system of forms, a different administrative track, and hundreds of other petty, ridiculous, and tedious details that make for one hugely inefficient system that is supposed to be enforcing and interpreting the same law.

In federal courts, it is even worse: Each petty tyrant and "chief judge" wants his own brand of genius forever emblazoned on every mindless form that must be filled out, and on every useless rule that must be followed. The result is that a litigant needs to take a whole course in the "Local Rules of Court" of whatever jurisdiction he is so unlucky as to find himself in.

Because the courts cannot handle this overflowing deluge of cases, the court officials have resorted to a truncated system, whereby the basic goal of every judge is to settle every case and to avoid trials at all costs. Indeed, trials are treated like the Black Plague; they are something to be shunned and avoided at any cost.

To avoid their dreaded *bête noire*, The Trial, judges have converted their courts into mass assembly lines in which the end product is a "settlement" between the plaintiff and defendant. In addition, courthouses all across the land have vastly accelerated the pace of lawsuit processing, have required a form of "alternative dispute resolution" (ADR) such as mediation or arbitration in every case, and have tried to get every case "resolved" within one year of its filing.

This massive acceleration of the tempo of litigation clearly works to the plaintiffs' advantage. In the old days, stodgy corporate defendants could drag out cases for five, ten, or twenty years by endless procedural delay mechanisms in order to avoid paying plaintiffs. Today, they no longer enjoy that luxury. (The catch is that the plaintiff must now avoid the equally dangerous outcome of summary judgment. But more of that later.)

Statistics show that over 96 percent of all cases filed in court all over the country are settled before trial. The few cases that do make it to trial are likely to sputter out in interminable and tedious arcana of the law that is beyond the understanding of even the most erudite juries.

Judges all follow "Judge Grumpy's Law," in which the name of the game is to "decide" (terminate) a case or forcing a settlement.

Typically, a court will schedule a "mandatory settlement conference" (MSC) in every case, the earlier the better. In that MSC, a judge, hitherto totally unfamiliar with the case, will seek to "bring the two sides together" to work out a deal that both can live with. The judge will generally try to persuade the defendants that it would be monstrously expensive to try a case. He will then switch gears (in a different caucus room) and try to manipulate a plaintiff into believing that he does not have a strong case and must settle in order to avoid paying "court costs and fees."

Because the settlement judge is so inundated with cases that he has no time to read them, what is said in the MSC may not bear the slightest relation to truth or reality. The judge is blind to this fact: He cares only to settle the case and "clear his calendar." A typical law and motion judge will handle as many as thirty or forty cases in a day. Although the judge does have clerks and research assistants, for anyone to penetrate that morass with an actual legal point may be nearly impossible.

Indeed, "clearing the calendar" has become the main goal of most judges nowadays. Again, judges are in the disposal business. They tend to see the ultimate facts of cases as a blur and, more often than not, do not even read papers presented before them.

I once tried an experiment in which I filed a brief with a judge, in which I attached a cover sheet and pages of the Bible. To my amazement and shock, the judge didn't even read the brief and proceeded to process the case like a blind man groping his way around. Next time, I just copied a telephone book. The result was the same: no comment.

Recently, I found myself in a courtroom filled with 200 lawyers set for ninety cases, all of whom had a case scheduled at the same time: 9:00 A.M. in the same courtroom. This resembled a "cattle call" more than a courtroom, and the only thing the judge did was to assign cases to mediation.

An uneducated cretin with a room temperature IQ could just as easily have done this job. So it is no wonder that the quality of our judges has deteriorated so far.

As the judge performs best the Settlement Dance—where the blind lead the blind and the only goal is "Let's Make a Deal"—it is small wonder that the Settlement Conference is generally a con game. The con game is that the judge says different things to each side separately and leans on both sides to compromise and go away.

In such an atmosphere, stapling excerpts from the Holy Bible to a brief has more weight than citing obscure cases, all of which obey Newton's First Law of the Law anyway: "For each opinion, there is an equal and opposite opinion."

The fact that the Settlement Dance works in 96 percent of

all case shows how this process favors the plaintiff-litigant, that is, he who strikes first.

In other words, because of the statistics and the courts' inability to seriously handle even a tiny portion of their cases through "trial," you have a darn good chance of winning some money just by the act of filing suit.

The lawsuit today is the closest thing to a free lunch that Americans have, though most of them do not realize this because of the thicket of legalese mumbo-jumbo and the elaborate masquerade going on in the House of Judges. So sue your creditor and win big!

THE DEFENDANT: EVEN WHEN HE WINS, HE LOSES

To drive this point home, I like to recite the "Clint Eastwood Law of the Law," which was recently proven in federal court in San Jose. Eastwood, the world-famous movie star and multimillionaire owner of the Mission Inn in Carmel, California, was sued by a customer for failing to install an elevator in his motel. Being Dirty Harry in real life as in films, Clint defied the plaintiff, refused to settle with her, and challenged her to *"MAKE MY DAY"* by dragging the case out to a full-blown jury trial, in federal court in San Jose.

The plaintiff *did* make Clint's day, but not exactly as the movie star had imagined. The lengthy trial, which cost Eastwood much time and millions of dollars in his own money paid to his own defense lawyers, resulted in a verdict for the lady customer, and against Eastwood for violation of federal laws forbidding discrimination against the handicapped by public establishments, such as motels.

Though the jury voted for the plaintiff, it found that she had "no real monetary damages." Yet, because she was the "prevailing party" in the trial, technically speaking, Eastwood was ordered by the judge to pay her more than $600,000 anyway, in her attorney fees and costs, including costs of expert witnesses, trial exhibits, and so on.

It is easy to see from this example that even the most frivolous plaintiffs, who suffer no real compensatory monetary damages at all, can bring a behemoth defendant to his knees just by the mere fact of dragging him through the courts for years.

It is this singular fact, contained in "Clint Eastwood's Law of the Law," that encourages defendants to settle all cases in order to avoid a costly trial, regardless of the outcome and underlying merits of the lawsuit. I happened to be in the federal courthouse that day, when the verdict and its $600,000-plus price tag were announced. The plaintiff's lawyer was all smiles while poor Dirty Harry was nowhere to be found. Clint Eastwood's movie roles are generally heroic. But there is nothing heroic about this story.

Thus, with the mathematics working against defendants, and with armies of black robes prodding them like cattle to enter the Settlement Stable, how can a debtor-plaintiff ever lose? The system is inherently biased in favor of anyone who strikes first by filing suit first.

The House of Judges is truly a house of cards. It is based on illusion, sleight of hand, skullduggery, fraud, pretense, egomania, mindless ceremony, and inexorable mathematical and economic laws that dictate an outcome in favor of the plaintiff in the vast majority of cases.

No wonder people overseas are now overheard saying, "I want to go to America and sue somebody; the courthouses are made of gold."

22

ESCAPING THE "SUMMARY JUDGMENT" MONSTER

WHILE THE OBSESSION judges have with "clearing their calendars" serves the plaintiff's interests, insofar as it encourages the parties to "SETTLE, SETTLE, SETTLE," there is also a dark side to this instant-disposal mentality.

Because judges are overwhelmingly concerned only with sweeping away cases, they tend to dismiss a lot of cases by a method that is arguably unconstitutional (in violation of the Seventh Amendment to the U.S. Constitution). This most certainly results in the practical consignment of many (but not all) plaintiffs to second-class citizenship. Nevertheless this system, called the Motion for Summary Judgment System, or MSJ, consigns many an unwary litigant into the dust heap of court history.

THE GENESIS OF THE SUMMARY JUDGMENT MOTION

The MSJ monster is the bugaboo of all plaintiffs, and is that most singular device for strangling the plaintiff's case at the throat and preventing it from going to trial. This is a method that truncates a case, cuts off the plaintiff's legs at the knees, and prevents his case from ever getting before a jury of his fellow citizens.

A strong case can be made that this MSJ system is unconstitutional because it violates the Seventh Amendment of the U.S. Constitution, which gives every American citizen the right to go to trial in any civil controversy where the amount in dispute "exceeds ten dollars." This right to due process was intended by our forefathers as a guarantee of equality before the law for each citizen. Yet a well-financed defendant can erect a practical barrier that will prevent most citizens from obtaining redress of grievances in the courts via MSJ.

Yet because of the growth of the MSJ monster in recent years, as a direct response to the massive increase in lawsuits, people's rights are being violated every day by the very black robes who have sworn to uphold them.

The MSJ is a device that came about to be used as an abusive tool of disposal by cynical black robes only in the past twenty years or so. The MSJ, which appears in the rules of civil procedure of every state court and the federal courts as well, provides that "if there are no material facts in dispute between the parties," the judge can dismiss the case at any point in the proceedings. This is a decision on the case as a matter of law that is up to the judge alone, and it does not involve a jury.

HOW THE MONSTER WORKS: TRIAL BY PAPER

The MSJ works as follows: Highly-paid defense lawyers prepare a monster of a motion that is at least two inches thick and may be as large as an entire file box. This monster motion is filled with hundreds of pages of briefs and affidavits, in which it is argued that "there are no material facts in dispute between plaintiff and defendant," and so they contend they should win the case *eo instante*, as a legal right. They argue that there is no need for a trial, since a black robe can determine that there are no factual disputes.

MSJ is the killing ground of every plaintiff's case, the booby trap to be avoided. It might be called the "Pacman" of the courts, for it gobbles up cases and throws the unwary plaintiff out of court in an instant.

The trick is to force a settlement before MSJ is invoked. This point is usually found after a few depositions have been taken and the defendants have just enough facts to obscure the story of the case. If a way to settlement cannot be found, then it becomes necessary for the under-funded plaintiff to find a way to oppose MSJ by submitting affidavits from witnesses asserting that a dispute of a material fact exists.

MSJ is inherently unfair. It favors the defendants in all cases because they have almost unlimited time and financial resources to put together a massive motion for summary judgment. Then the plaintiff has only two weeks in which to prepare an opposition. This monstrous disparity in preparation time is clearly unconstitutional and amounts to a denial of the right to a trial. But the black robes don't give a damn. All they care about is clearing their calendars, and the MSJ offers them an easy way to do that.

MSJ is theoretically available to plaintiffs as well as defendants. But the object for a plaintiff is to get his case before a jury. As a practical matter, over 90 percent of all MSJs are filed and won by defendants. So it is really a defendant's tool.

MSJ IN THE HANDS OF CREDITORS

The power of this tool in the hands of an aggressive defendant really comes into its own in debt litigation. In the context of debt litigation, where a creditor-collector may be the plaintiff suing the debtor-defendant, MSJ is likely to be used as soon as the case is filed. The collector will argue in umpteen affidavits that the debtor signed the credit agreement, promised to pay, defaulted, and should lose "as a matter of law."

In opposing such an MSJ, the debtor-defendant should argue that there are material facts in dispute as to the defects in the creditor's performance. For example, the debtor should file affidavits proving that the products or services charged were somehow defective, and that whether or not they were defective is "a material issue of fact in dispute," so the case should go to trial, where a jury can decide.

If the debtor files enough affidavits and brings up at least one issue of fact in dispute, he may be able to defeat the MSJ. That is why it is so important for the debtor to file a cross-complaint or counterclaim against the creditor and all his agents, to assert that such material issues of fact truly exist. If a black robe sees that a counterclaim is on file, he is more likely to deny a defendant's motion for summary judgment.

Many corporate litigants (i.e., creditors) take a hard line stance when a case begins, and tell the debtor that they will not even negotiate a settlement "until after MSJ." Sometimes this is a bluff, but there is an inherent conflict of interest between creditor-attorneys and their clients. The attorney has a vested interest in earning as much money as he can by dragging out the case and charging his client more and more money, while the creditor client has an interest in limiting the amount of legal fees paid. Thus, there is an inherent limited opportunity for the debtor to form a *de facto* alliance with the creditor's lawyer. By filing endless interrogatories, taking endless depositions, and otherwise dragging out the case, the corporate counsel shares the debtor's interest in dragging out the case. This helps forestall or at least delay the Monster of Summary Judgment, and it can help in negotiating a settlement of the dispute.

In settlement conferences and mediations, judges insist that a representative of the creditor-litigant be present, because they realize there is an inherent conflict between lawyer and client in this area. The black robes want the case "resolved" so they can clear their calendars, and so they force the actual parties to confront each other.

If the debtor-plaintiff cannot win a case based on its merits, or senses that defeat is near via MSJ, he may still be able to negotiate a settlement with the creditor. But usually, he can fight off the MSJ if he gets the right affidavits from witnesses, including himself. Many laymen don't understand that the debtor himself is a "witness," and that his testimony is entitled to be called "evidence" per se; this permits him to assert the material issues in dispute.

What often happens, as a practical matter, is that the litigant is often put in such a tangled position that he misses the proverbial forest for the trees. The debtor-plaintiff may become so obsessed with the sheer volume of paperwork filed in the case, and with the emotions of the hour, that he cannot understand that all he needs to do is to assert material issues of fact in dispute.

I had one case in which a Native American woman filed a countersuit against a creditor on a school loan default, in which she asserted that she was being discriminated against on the basis of race because she was expelled. It should have been a good suit. She borrowed money in order to receive an education and then, either allegedly through discrimination or not, she did not get that education. If she flunked out of school because she was not qualified, it is arguable that she should not have been admitted and the school only admitted her to get her money. In any case, where is the value received?

However, this woman failed to assert in her affidavits and depositions even one solid fact that would create an issue of fact in dispute on whether racial discrimination had occurred. As a consequence, she went down for the count on MSJ. She then came to me to do an appeal, as she was facing $300,000 in student loans, after being kicked out of the school and receiving nothing for her efforts.

LIFE AFTER MSJ:
THE LONG-TERM PROSPECTS

The Native American woman's sad case illustrates the problem with failing to understand the nature of the MSJ beast. Litigants are thrown out of court and then desperately seek to file appeals, but by the time they find a lawyer for the appeal, it is often too late, because the appellate court will be bound by the record that was presented before the lower court. A crucial fact, which is often realized too late, is that new evidence cannot be admitted at the appellate level. Appeals courts cannot consider facts that were not presented before the lower court.

The result was that her suit was not salvageable. But with foresight and proper planning in the early stages, it should have been a good suit. The "Pacman" of MSJ gobbles another one.

23

CRIMINAL LAW: THE MODERN-
DAY DEBTOR'S PRISON

SO FAR IN THIS BOOK, we have discussed only civil law: suits and countersuits between private parties, the creditor and the debtor. While civil law is the main forum in which creditor busting takes place, we cannot ignore that other parallel universe hovering in the background: criminal law.

Like everything else in this business, criminal law offers the litigant the proverbial double-edged sword. It can be used for you or against you. The point is to recognize the danger points and opportunity points, and to act in your own best interest.

Technically, criminal law always involves the government against a private party. In state law, the government is represented by the District Attorney (DA) of each state and county. In the federal system, the prosecutor is called the "U.S. Attorney."

Although private people have the legal right to make a "citizen's arrest" of a wrongdoer, they do not have the legal standing to bring a criminal action against that wrongdoer in court. Only the DA and the U.S. Attorney have that exclusive right.

THE HISTORY OF THE DOUBLE-EDGED SWORD

In the good old days of Merry Olde England, where the U.S. legal system was born, the criminal law pitted "The Crown" against debtors, and the system was always anti-debtor. "The Crown" was represented by "My Lord" the prosecutor, a government agent who invariably threw the book at anyone accused of defaulting on a debt. Indeed, debtors were regularly charged with a crime against "The Crown," and were normally thrown into debtor's prison until they could pay their debts to their creditors. "The Crown" acted as Super Collector for creditors. Many debtors never got out of prison alive.

Anyone familiar with Charles Dickens's scathing novels about the British social and penal system in the nineteenth century knows the reputation of the infamous debtor's prison. The idea of the debtor's prison was so infamous that it was the paradigm of what we now call the "Catch-22" before there was a *Catch-22*. If someone is in prison until he pays off his debt and yet he can't work to make money to pay the debt while in prison, he has what amounts to an infinite sentence for a minor offense.

The debtor's prison was transplanted from the mother country to the United States in the early decades of our country's existence. It eventually found itself cast into the ash heap of history and condemned as an "inhumane" and irrational procedure for hounding debtors.

"The Crown" also seized the property of "convicted" debtors and used that to pay off their debts. The point is that it was a crime against the state for anyone to refuse to pay his creditor.

Today, our system of "justice" has evolved greatly, but there are still subtle remnants of the debtor's prison system that can be found hidden under rocks of our judicial system.

While no debtor can be imprisoned today just for defaulting

on a debt, as a practical matter one's creditors can "appeal" to prosecutors (both state and federal) to go after a debtor by accusing him or her of "criminal fraud, of a criminal intent to deceive the creditor." This leads to the natural question: What exactly is "criminal fraud," as opposed to "civil fraud"?

It's time to trot out old Einstein and a slight variation on his Law of Relativity here: "Criminally fraudulent intent is in the eye of the beholder."

It is really up to a prosecutor's discretion to decide whether a debtor acted with "sufficiently evil intent" as to form the legal state of mind needed to charge him with criminal fraud. It is a fact that creditors, being wealthy and influential persons and financial institutions, often have the ear of a particular prosecutor. After all, it is these wealthy creditors who often finance the political campaigns of prosecutors. If a prosecutor, after consultation with the representatives of a wealthy creditor, can be persuaded that a debtor never intended to pay back his loan when he obtained the loan from his creditors, the prosecutor can file a criminal complaint against the debtor, and thus throw him into the clutches of the parallel universe of criminal law.

There is no clear demarcation between civil and criminal intent, but the debtor needs to have a clean paper trail so that his tracks are covered. A debtor needs to be aware of this danger and to be prepared before he embarks on a campaign of creditor-busting.

THE GAME OF INFLUENCE IN CRIMINAL PROSECUTION

All state and county DAs are elected politicians who run for office, are politically ambitious, and rely on creditors and other fat cats to finance their political campaigns. If your creditor has a close political or financial tie to the political puppet who serves as your friendly local prosecutor, *watch out!* You may get hit with criminal charges if you default on your debt, or if you say the wrong thing.

In the federal system, assistant U.S. attorneys are appointed by the President and U.S. Attorney General of the United States in Washington. They are not elected. So, unless the President and his pals have close financial and political ties to your friendly local creditor, you are safer from prosecution in the federal system than you are in the state. Indeed, the federal system was supposed to have been designed by the founding fathers in such a manner as to insulate criminal law from politics, and to prevent Rockefeller's Law of the Law from taking effect. Unfortunately, their system is not perfect, and we often see ambitious local politicos *qua* U.S. attorneys going after debtors criminally, just because creditors want them to.

In addition to criminal fraud, debtors in default need to beware of being hit with criminal charges of "perjury" and related crimes,. These can include "making a false statement on a loan application" (a federal crime) and making "false statements to law enforcement officers," such as local street cops and FBI agents. (Making a false statement to an FBI agent is a federal felony punishable by ten years in the slammer; copycat state statutes are equally Draconian.) Yes, the debtor's prison is alive and well in our society today, except that it operates under different guises.

If you feel you have been wrongfully charged with a crime, the first step is to get yourself a good criminal lawyer, a courtroom brawler who will take the fight to the limit. In criminal law, as in civil law, courthouses are overcrowded with cases, and judges follow Judge Grumpy's Law and seek mainly to clear their calendars. (Although some state judges are elected and are puppets of creditors who finance their campaigns.)

The last thing you want to do, if accused of a crime, is to sign onto a "public defender," a mindless drone paid peanuts by the court to railroad his clients into guilty pleas. In general, you need to hire a brawler who will fight on your behalf.

To gain a conviction in criminal law, the prosecutor must convince a jury unanimously that you are "guilty beyond a reasonable doubt." Despite its being discussed in countless TV and movie courtroom dramas, no one has yet been able to explain what "reasonable doubt" really means. Indeed, the courtroom dramas are usually centered around everyone's inability to define it. "Reasonable doubt" is an utterly meaningless concept that means whatever a particular judge or jury *thinks* it means.

Nonetheless, many jurors take their tasks seriously and will not convict if a defendant seems to be a nice person. Hence, prosecutors do not like to charge people with financial or related crimes unless they feel they can win a conviction. Ninety-five percent of all criminal cases result in either dismissal of charges or a plea bargain. These statistics are a close parallel to their civil case counterparts.

And as in the civil arena, the best defense is a strong offense. If you are charged with crime, you should consider suing the prosecutor and his creditor cohorts in *civil* court for false arrest, false imprisonment, malicious prosecution, abuse of process, and myriad other causes of action.

In some jurisdictions, you can pursue a civil case simultaneously with the criminal case against you. It will serve to jack up the legal fees and costs of the prosecutors, may reveal embarrassing things about the prosecutors' unholy alliance with creditors, and may win you a dismissal of charges or acquittal.

In general, whenever charged with a crime, a defendant-debtor should consider suing the prosecutor and police, as well as the creditors who put them into play, in civil court. I call this the "Vince Lombardi Law of the Law," which holds that "Winning isn't everything; it's the only thing: so when hit with a criminal suit, sue the prosecutor in civil court."

You can sue not only the prosecutor, but also the police,

FBI agents, and any other government official who has done you wrong, and you can put them all in the same stew with the creditors, their co-defendants, and allies.

THE TRUTH ABOUT PERJURY

Apart from the strategy of fighting a criminal case, we need to consider what exactly is involved in the crime of perjury. Perjury is always a felony, so you need to avoid it by always telling the truth. That is, you cannot deliberately and intentionally lie, because if you do so, that is perjury. Perjury is not simply a matter of "lying under oath," however. In most jurisdictions, this crime is defined as "lying under oath *on a material fact in a case.*" That is, if you lie on an immaterial fact, it's not perjury. So your first line of defense is to argue that what is at issue was not a material fact (material to the case at hand, that is). If, for example, you lie under oath by asserting that the San Francisco Giants won the World Series in 1962 (they did not), and this has nothing to do with your case against your creditor, your untrue assertion is not perjury, even though it is technically a lie under oath. But if the lawsuit concerns ownership of a 1962 Giants-Yankees World Series item of memorabilia, and you lie as to who won the Series, your lie could constitute perjury because that fact may be material to the particular case at issue.

It should not be forgotten that perjury is not confined to courtroom testimony. In fact, if you get embroiled in a civil or criminal lawsuit, you will have to sign numerous affidavits and declarations "under penalty of perjury" and file them with the court. If you borrow money for a mortgage or other loan from a creditor, you may sign documents "under penalty of perjury" regarding your financial status, the purpose of the loan, etc. If you borrow $100,000 from Bank A by signing documents saying you want the cash for home improvements, and then use the loan proceeds to play the stock market, you can be charged with perjury and with crimes of making false statements to get a loan, and with criminal fraud.

So, watch what you sign. Though studies show that less than 3 percent of all borrowers ever read the hundreds of pages of tedious forms they are required to sign in order to get a loan, it behooves you to read all the gobbledygook in order to avoid a perjury rap later on in the case.

It should also be pointed out that if you file a civil suit or countersuit against a creditor, you will encounter the risk of perjury repeatedly, because you will have to sign statements and orally make statements under oath, in depositions, trials, motions, etc. It is absolutely crucial that everyone be aware of the risks and not expose oneself to the charge of perjury.

In most states and in federal court, you don't have to verify the facts asserted in a civil lawsuit (complaint) under penalty of perjury, but ultimately you may have to testify under oath on the witness stand or in written declarations.

While prosecutors rarely charge civil litigants with perjury for statements made in or outside a court proceeding (unless the evidence of perjury is overwhelming and there is political pressure to bear), perjury is always a sword of Damocles hanging over every litigant's head. So, the upshot of all this is: Check out your facts, be careful with your statements, and know the evidence. It is not sufficient to be honest. It is also necessary to be informed and careful in order to protect oneself against the charge of perjury.

KEEP YOUR WITS ABOUT YOU

Criminal law is a nasty business. When people are formally charged with a crime, arrested, put in handcuffs, ridiculed by being forced to walk the "perp walk" before television cameras, they generally feel as if they have been hit by a ten-ton truck. Most people confronted with these circumstances are overwhelmed with feelings of fear and shame. They lose control of their lives. They fear being thrown in jail with rapists, child molesters, dopers, and murderers. They fear sexual and physical assault in prison, and they fear that they may never be able to get a good job or be accepted in society again. As a result of this pressure, criminal defendants usually panic and cop a guilty plea in the early innings of the game. Prosecutors know this and use it to their advantage.

But copping a plea—especially in the early innings—is almost always a serious and totally unnecessary mistake. The goal of the criminal defendant, as with the civil debtor-litigant, must always be to stretch the game into extra innings—twenty, thirty, or fifty innings, if possible. This is done until the prosecutor gives up, and drops the charges or offers you a good plea to a trivial crime, such as an infraction for "disturbing the peace," or something equally innocuous.

The best thing is to be aware of your surroundings, your statements, and of the forms you sign, and to be honest about what you say and write. That way, you need not compound your problems by being thrown into the debtor's prison parallel universe.

I have seen unscrupulous creditors hound prosecutors to persecute innocent debtors, ascribing to them malicious criminal intent, just so the creditors can shake down their insurance companies to pay off the bad debt. Many creditors hold insurance policies, whereby insurance companies will become obligated to pay them their losses in bad debts if the creditors can demonstrate that their debtors "committed a crime" or borrowed money on criminally fraudulent pretenses. This rule gives creditors a strong motive to bring prosecutors into play, by urging them to accuse the defaulting debtors of crimes.

I once had a case where a forty-eight-year-old RV salesman—with no previous criminal record and sterling prior credit—was accused of criminal fraud by RV lenders, and was hounded by the FBI for five years after the alleged crimes took place. He was convicted and sent to prison for twenty-five years, without any chance of parole. Meanwhile, the RV lenders recovered handsomely on their insurance policies.

This was a classic debtor's prison case. The unfortunate RV man made some mistakes along the way, such as failing to accept a generous plea bargain offer (plea to one count of misdemeanor, no jail time, and pay a $500 fine). He went the distance, got convicted of twenty-five counts of felony fraud, and said hello to the slammer for twenty-five years.

Anyone can be charged with crimes. No one is immune. The clever debtor would do well to tread carefully and be alert to anything that might send him to the other side of the tracks of the criminal justice system.

Expert Witnesses for Hire: Pied Pipers of the Courts

EXPERT WITNESSES ARE among the most misunderstood and yet most valuable players in the game of creditor-busting litigation. In today's high-tech world, the expert witness is actually more important than the percipient lay witness in many cases—especially in those involving technological gadgetry, such as vehicles, machines, computers, and the like.

What is an expert witness, anyway? To find out, go to your local bar association or library and pick up a copy of the *Directory of Experts.* Or write to the American Trial Lawyers Association or the Trial Lawyers Association in your state. Expert witnesses are those men and women whose professional training, experience, and background qualify them to be certified as "expert witnesses" if a case goes to trial.

Experts: An Opinion for Every Occasion

Despite sanctimonious assertions to the contrary, the stark truth is that in our legal system, all experts are for sale. All experts follow Newton's First Law of the Law and Einstein's Law of Relativity, for they know that almost any factual situation can be interpreted in contradictory opinions that are for sale. The "Law of Expert Sale" is that you hire the expert, and you pay him a fee to support your case and testify for your side. Though courts and experts do not state this fact openly, this Law of Expert Sale is what makes the legal world go around. This is how the system works. An expert opinion is just another commodity for sale to the highest bidder.

The expert witness has far greater credibility with judges and juries than do the lay witnesses who actually saw what happened, in most cases. For an expert to have the title of "Doctor" before his or her name is to elevate himself or herself into a rarefied plane of human achievement. Because most jurors are not "doctors" and don't even have a college sheepskin, they tend to be star-struck by any expert witness. They tend to believe the expert not because of *what* he says, but because of *who* he is.

If your expert witness can just sow the seeds of "reasonable doubt" as to whether a car or computer or machine works properly, or whether the medical creditors committed malpractice, or whether your unfriendly creditor committed fraud or breach of contract or the like, you are more than halfway to winning your case.

Experts can be "rented" and "bought" for fees ranging from $100 per hour to $1,000 per hour, with retainers ranging from $1,500 to millions of dollars, but the cost is well worth it, if the expert can help you to get out of a bad debt situation.

The expert witness is the only witness known to God and man who is allowed to render an "opinion" in a court of law. Lay witnesses are not allowed to do that. The expert witness is the only witness allowed to answer and assert a "hypothetical opinion." The expert can so tie up the minds of jurors and counsel that it will take them days, if not years, to understand what he has said in technocratic mumbo jumbo.

Yes, the expert is definitely worth it.

Most government technical workers, such as firemen, policemen, scientists, lab techs, regulatory officers and the like, dream of one day retiring from their public servant job and going into a much more lucrative "private sector" job as an expert witness and consultant. Show me a retired big city fire chief or police chief and I will show you a future expert witness for hire. Show me a retired state or county inspection officer, and I will show you an expert witness for hire.

Experts are not hard to find, and they are easy to hire. They are the magic genies of any case. They can greatly increase your chances of winning or settling a suit based on your allegations that a house or vehicle or computer or other good or service was defective, or that your creditor defrauded you. They are your ticket to wiping out a $50,000 medical bill by asserting that the medical care you received was substandard malpractice.

Expert witnesses exist in every field, and carry a veneer of neutrality, but in fact, they are always biased in favor of the party who pays their fees.

The "Pied Piper Law of the Law" holds that "He who pays the Piper calls the tune," the tune to which the rats march. There can be no question that experts are pied pipers, and that jurors and judges—like the legendary rats of Hamlin fame—follow the experts blindly, while you call the tune if you pay these pipers their fees.

If you want to stop that car from being seized by the Repo Man, hire an expert witness to allege that the car was defective or that the dealer defrauded you. If you want to avoid being bankrupted by a greedy doctor or hospital, hire a medical expert witness to allege that the treatment was defective, that you are a victim of malpractice. If you want to avoid paying a

$25,000 legal fee to a lawyer-drone, hire an expert witness to opine that the legal advice fell short of the professional standards. That last one is the hardest, of course, because what constitutes legal advice is so flexible and subjective and the attorney institutions are so inbred. But that may not matter in terms of the results of the suit. The point is to hire the expert, then wait for the result.

BREAKING WITH THE PROFESSIONAL BROTHERHOOD

As a general rule, expert witnesses are easier to find in your local area for purely technical areas than for "professional" areas such as medicine or law. You can find an expert in automotive science in your hometown far easier than you can find a legal or medical expert for hire.

To find professional experts, such as doctors or lawyers, you often have to go outside the city limits—sometimes out of state—because these professional experts follow an "Honor among Thieves" rule. As so-called "professionals," they tend to avoid testifying against one of their local "colleagues" for fear that the bad guy will retaliate by testifying against them, in a future case where their own hide is on the line. Not only that, but there is also a social price to pay when your expert sees his target at the next professional meeting or luncheon. And the experts' wives may know each other. Such situations can get very sticky, very quickly. That is over and above the natural stick-together mentality that they tend to have.

Apart from this "Law of Distances," you can find expert witnesses easily.

Even in a lawsuit as seemingly straightforward as racial or age discrimination, you need an expert witness to divine the intent of the defendant in discriminating. The expert would review statistical as well as anecdotal data, and he would conclude his investigation with an opinion based on whatever you want him to say—as long as you pay his fee and as long as there is some arguable basis for his opinion.

So, you say that you don't want to pay that nasty contractor $100,000 for remodeling your house or building? No problem, just call experts for hire. You can find an expert witness eager to testify that the contractor's work was defective, and you can skate home free—or almost free.

Another thing to realize about experts is that their fees generally must be paid up front. But those same fees are "recoverable" if and when you win your case. That is, the expert witness offers you yet another billy club with which to clobber your creditor opponent, and force him to settle the debt. The minute you put an expert witness into play, the creditor must realize that he could be on the line for paying your expert's fees, generally to the tune of thousands of dollars more.

Yes, it is small wonder that the expert witness is an essential tool within today's technocratic-society courtroom.

25

Sealing the Deal: Suing Your Way to a Clean Credit History

NO MATTER HOW WELL one uses the techniques in this book, one thing must remain at the back of every debtor's mind: how to clean up bad credit during or after the litigation fireworks.

All right, you say, so you can battle creditors until they cave in, but what about the smell of bad credit that they leave behind? Isn't that going to stay on your "record" forever? How in the world are you even going to get credit again? What sane creditor, knowing of your creditor-busting record, would even hand you a credit card for the rest of your life? What will you do about that abysmally low FICO credit score of 500, on a scale of 0 to 1,000?

The most important credit "score" for every consumer is the so-called FICO score, which stands for "Fair Isaacs and Company" Score. It is a score ranging from 0 to 1,000. Due to the mindless herd mentality of corporate America, every creditor bows down and worships the Golden Calf of FICO, and makes credit and interest rate determinations based mainly on this dubious tabulation. The parameters determining a debtor's FICO score include not only his debt-paying history, but also such mindless intangibles as the total number of credit checks on him that have been run by various sundry merchants, whether there has been a significant and recent diminution in total outstanding debt, and other dubious and amorphous parameters. FICO scores and explanations can be found at the Web site *www.fairisaac.com*. But there is nothing "fair" about this matter.

LETTERS FROM THE CREDITOR WIPE THE SLATE CLEAN

How then can a defaulting debtor be "born again"? The question is a fair one, yet it is surprisingly simple to answer. Whenever you enter the arena of settlement with your creditor foes, you must always insist that as part of the settlement agreement, they must write letters to all credit reporting bureaus and FICO, instructing them to remove all derogatory credit reports from your record, or else there is no deal. Don't forget that this is one of the main reasons why you sued or countersued your creditors in the first place, in other words, for credit libel and slander.

It is surprising how relatively simple this rule is, and yet how few debtor-litigants bother to invoke it. I call it the "Janitor's Law of the Law," for it holds that as part of any settlement with a creditor, you must insist that your bad credit be cleaned up. The creditor has got to call out the cleanup crew, or there is no deal.

The Janitor's Law of the Law is surprisingly easy to put into operation, because it costs the creditor next to nothing to write a letter to TRW, FICO, and the other credit agencies, instructing them that the debt was in dispute and has now been settled and that there has been "full satisfaction" of the debt and that it was all just a simple misunderstanding. If FICO and TRW don't erase the bad marks and raise your credit rating, you can threaten to sue *them* for credit libel.

Creditors don't give a damn about what happens to you vis-à-vis other unknown creditors *in futuro*. All they care about is resolving their expensive dispute with you here and now. Thus, if you insist on invoking the Janitor's Law as a "deal breaker" to any settlement, and all other things being equal, you will win at least 99 percent of the time.

There are always going to be a handful of "Puritan" creditors out there who believe that a bad debtor should be "reported" and have his credit history blackened forever, as punishment for what they consider to be "bad and immoral character and debt-evasion practices." But you should rest assured that these Puritans are few and far between, and that they are usually just bluffing and using credit cleanup as a purported bargaining chip in the settlement negotiations.

Before your creditor foes surrender in a settlement ceremony, always be sure to see a copy of their proposed letter to the credit bureaus first. Because the bureaus operate in a Kafkaesque no-man's-land and are inscrutable and totally unresponsive bureaucrats who never come out and talk to you openly, you have to be sure that your foe has signed over the letter instructing them to erase your bad debt marks.

Otherwise, you are to shout, "NO DEAL!"

Of course, if you win the lottery and need not worry about getting credit for the rest of your life, you don't need to bring out the Janitor armies. But for most of us ordinary mortals, who thrive on plastic as mosquitoes feast on blood, you will need to apply for future credit, and you don't want to face future creditors with a bad credit score or rating.

CONFIDENTIALITY: THE OTHER SOURCE OF CLEAN CREDIT

It is true that anyone can always look up your litigation record on file at any court, since this is a public document. But in general, settlement agreements must be held confidential, and there must be a confidentiality clause inserted in the agreement, forbidding either side from ever revealing to any third parties any of the terms of the settlement or the facts of the case. This is standard procedure and must be followed to the hilt. That way, no future creditor or employer or landlord will ever be able to know what really happened. Nor should they know, for they have no right to know, as it is none of their business.

As a practical matter, 99.9 percent of all litigation settlement agreements have confidentiality clauses, where money changes hands (or the creditor cancels your debt) in the settlement process, so lawyers expect the confidentiality clause as par for the course. It is in the creditor's self-interest to keep the terms of settlement confidential, because no creditor wants any other debtors out there to become aware of the fact that the creditor is a "pushover" who canceled the debt of another debtor.

Hence, you have a built-in safeguard in the process whereby the creditors must realize it is in their own self-interest to keep the terms of settlement confidential, because they do not want to encourage an avalanche of lawsuits by other debtors encouraged by your success.

Nonetheless, because nothing is certain in the law and because creditors sometimes have idiots or thieves for lawyers and principals, you cannot assume anything and must always insist on a confidentiality clause as part of the settlement agreement.

Apart from the confidentiality clause and the Janitor's cleanup requirement, is there anything else that must be inserted in a settlement agreement? Settlement agreements sometimes have what is called a "liquidated damages" provision. This means that a specific dollar amount is inserted in a clause, requiring that if either party breaches any term of the agreement (such as the confidentiality clause), that guilty party must pony up a specific amount of money as punishment and as incentive not to spill the beans to John Q. Public. The liquidated damages can be anything (here there is no rule—following the Entropy Law of the Law, it is all totally arbitrary). Typical liquidated damages clauses require anywhere from the amount of the original debt, or perhaps $5,000 to $20,000. This is negotiable.

My recommendation to you is to avoid liquidated damages provisions unless the amount of the penalty is reasonably small for your budget.

A settlement agreement is just another contract, and it follows ordinary contract law. One clause that creditors will try to insert in any settlement agreement is a provision providing that in the event of breach of contract (or, rather, allegations of breach) the law of a particular state shall be applied, and the winner shall get attorney fees and costs if he prevails in a court. Other settlement agreements provide for mandatory binding arbitration, which you should avoid like the plague (remember the pitfalls of arbitration, described earlier). As for a provision awarding attorney fees to the prevailing party in a future dispute, this is standard operating procedure for settlement agreements, though no sane debtor should like them. You should try to argue against them, but I would not treat this as a deal breaker.

You should insist that the law of your state be applied to interpret the agreement. You should also insist that the settlement agreement include a clause providing for "venue" to be in your home state court, if there is an allegation of breach of contract. Otherwise, you might be hauled into a court 3,000 miles away, forced to hire expensive lawyers, and to run your case *in absentia*.

All contracts can be disputed and can thus generate future disputes and future lawsuits, so be careful what you agree to. You may later regret what you signed, if you find yourself dragged into a court 3,000 miles away with a demand for your head on a platter, with attorney fees to boot.

Some creditors are unscrupulous and will follow "Franken-stein's Law" to purposefully draft settlement agreements in a cyn-ical manner, to take advantage of the naiveté of their debtor foes, with an eye toward creating a Frankenstein's Monster in the future and dragging you back into court with demands for your hide. Frankenstein's Law is something that you must avoid at all costs. Do not sign any settlement agreement that seems likely to bring you back into court under unfavorable circumstances.

To be safe, you should have a bona fide lawyer inspect any proposed settlement agreement, for he can probably red-flag any troublesome provision that is likely to sprout into a Frankenstein's Monster. You can usually find a "$25 lawyer" for hire for a half hour or hour of consultation by contacting any local bar association, who will assign you out to a drone for a minimal pro bono fee of $25 or so. Since America has 40 per-cent of all the world's lawyers, and there is a lawyer's office on every corner, you won't have any trouble finding a $25 drone. The drone's hope is that he can snatch you up as a paying client if he performs well for the $25, so he has an incentive to give you good advice. So don't hesitate to use this "free legal service" when faced with the final hurdle of your case, the set-tlement agreement.

In many ways, following "Napoleon's Law" ("History is written by the victors"), the settlement agreement will be the "history" of your case. Though it will be confidential, it will be something you can wear proudly, as far as you are concerned.

FUTURE LITIGATION: THE FRANKENSTEIN'S MONSTER OF SETTLEMENT

It is important that any settlement agreement not turn into a Frankenstein's Monster of future litigation. Many debtors feel "guilty" about "stiffing" the creditors, and experience pangs of guilt when it comes time to draw up the instrument of surrender.

They feel they have somehow "cheated" the creditor because they "borrowed money, got goods or services, and then walked away from their obligation to pay the piper."

Because of this misguided sense of guilt, which has utterly no place in the courtroom, guilt-laden debtors may be tempted to agree to unfavorable settlement agreements. This could surely doom them to face Frankenstein Monsters of future litigation on unfavorable terms, or doom them to be burdened with a bad credit history stigma for life.

If you feel guilty, see a priest or shrink. Do not let your feelings of guilt rub off on your negotiating and litigation strategy.

This maxim is called "Enron's Law of the Law": "There is no reason to feel guilty about stiffing a bad creditor, because you can safely assume that most creditors are as unethical as Enron executives, now that the true face of corporate America has been revealed." Since they would have no qualms about screwing you over and stealing your hard-earned money through dubious accounting and collection tricks. You should be confident in the fact that you have no reason to feel guilty.

Shedding the mantle of guilt, you should walk proudly into the settlement hall and insist on a settlement agreement that protects your interests. Do this while realizing that everybody will be glad the case is over and will go on to bigger and better things.

Whatever you do, don't let your guilt create a bad settlement agreement or a Frankenstein's monstrosity.

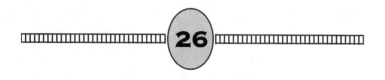

To Hire or Not
to Hire a Lawyer

IN THIS BOOK, I have often compared the filing of a lawsuit to "a magic bullet" and to "firing the shot heard 'round the world."

And in a fundamental sense, this is true.

Before a debtor files suit in court, he is seen by collectors and creditors as being "naked." He is viewed as undefended and helpless with no armor or weapons to counterstrike. Even the mere *threat* of a lawsuit is generally not enough to deter power-mad collectors, because it is viewed as a bluff. But once the suit is actually "filed and served," the magic bullet hits the head of the creditor beast, and suddenly the debtor is in a whole new ball game.

"FILE AND SERVE!" is what starts the clock ticking.

Everything we have said so far, about using litigation and counter-litigation as an effective tool against creditors, has begged one important issue: whether to hire or not to hire a lawyer.

How, you may ask, can a typical debtor afford a lawyer? What sense does it make to pay a stuffed-shirt mouthpiece $200 or more per hour to fight a creditor on a $5,000 bill? Is it possible to find a lawyer willing to work for free, or the next best thing, "on contingency"?

CLASS ACTION LAWYERS AND REPRESENTING YOURSELF

There is an old cliché that every lawyer hears somewhere along the line between law school and retirement: *He who represents himself has a fool for a client.*

If this adage is true for the lawyer, is it not even more true for the layman?

Representing oneself in court is a scary, nerve-wracking thing for most people uneducated in the intricacies of the law. But it need not be so. The truth is that the homily about having a fool for a client is self-serving from the legal profession's point of view. Landscape architects would like to convince us that you are a fool to design your own garden. Interior decorators would like to convince us that only a fool would buy his own furniture. What the legal profession won't tell you is that there can be a great deal of satisfaction in representing yourself in court. But what is even more basic is that you have an absolute *right* to do it yourself.

Anyone can file a lawsuit or countersuit in any court, and in fact, in some courts (typically, small claims courts), lawyers are banned.

Depending on the complexity and value of the debtor's case against the creditor, it may be possible to find a lawyer willing to work "on contingency" in representing the debtor. This means that the lawyer will agree to risk his time (and sometimes, if he is foolish or wealthy or very optimistic about the case, also his money on costs) in exchange for an agreement entitling him to win 33 percent or more of any settlement or verdict (some states limit the contingency percentage allowed; many states limit it depending on the type of case).

If the case is a class action, in theory, it will be easier to find lawyers willing to represent a debtor posing as a "lead plaintiff in a class action suit," because attorney fees are huge in such cases. For example, Bank of America has been sued successfully by class action lawyers fighting over the animus concerning the bank's charging of a $15 "late fee" for all Visa card payments received even a day late from debtors. Each individual case is probably worth no more than a few hundred dollars at best, but the combined total of 5 million plaintiff–credit card holders multiplies the damages into the millions. This means that the class action lawyer stands to win a fortune in legal fees if he prevails or settles the case.

There are many stories of class action lawyers who made instant fortunes mining in the quarry of class action suits. If a clever debtor can convince such a class action lawyer to take his case on contingency, the lawyer can indeed convert water into wine, transform base metal into gold. In the courtroom, "miracles" are indeed possible, because of the structure of the law.

Every major city has a cottage industry of class action lawyers, generally small or medium-sized firms who take on titans of industry. The debtor seeking to turn the scales against oppressive creditors can generally locate such class action lawyer firms by looking on the Internet, in old newspaper files, or at the local bar association or state bar.

Class action lawyers have sued airlines and airports over jet noise and the health hazards of secondhand smoke (a perfect suit or countersuit for a debtor seeking to combat an airline creditor, by the way), credit card user fees, monthly fees, late fees, and over-limit that had never been fully disclosed, etc. Class action superstars have scored against giants like Denny's, Texaco, Chase Manhattan, and the like—and their collection satellites and tentacles. There are lawyers who have scored against Lincoln Savings and McDonald's restaurants and who have built careers from their reputations that were subsequently generated.

But class action suits are not all that common, unless you find the magic bullet to shoot at the creditor, and it generally takes a pretty good and novel case to score a class action lawyer.

So, what about the debtor whose case does not have the sex appeal of such a suit? Can he find a lawyer?

Here the "Law of Legal Supply and Demand" comes into play: "Each year law schools churn out far more lawyers than can find real legal jobs in law firms, corporations, government agencies and the like." The Army of Unemployed and Under-employed Lawyers grows each year. In a country where "there is a lawyer on every street corner," the most litigious society in the history of the universe, how difficult can it be to find a barrister willing to go into court and fight for an aggrieved debtor?

Finding a lawyer is like panning for gold: The gold is there, but it may take some effort to find it. But because of the "Law of Excess of Lawyers," this can easily be done. By checking out legal newspapers, law schools, and local bar associations and their "referral services," it should be as easy to find a lawyer as it is to find a doctor.

But in many cases, a debtor may not be able to find a lawyer, so the only choice becomes to file suit *In Propria Persona* (In Pro Per).

To be an In Pro Per, at least for the onset of the case, one faces both good news and bad news. The bad news is that judges generally dislike In Pro Per litigants and regard them with some contempt; the good news is that judges and court clerks go much easier on the Pro Pers, allowing them far more leeway than they would a licensed pettifogger.

The Pro Per litigant can exploit this double standard by sending out waves of written discovery, costing his creditor opponent much money and legal fees in responding, while toiling for free with only his time to be thrown into the battle. This is no negligible advantage. Legal history is filled with stories of

Pro Per litigants who dragged down mighty corporate opponents, or sent them to the showers suing for peace.

My own view is that in our society, every high school and college in the country should give a mandatory course to all students, requiring them to learn the fundamentals of how to represent themselves in court. This course is like self-defense instruction: You just gotta know how to fight for yourself in court. I have given such courses through the Learning Annex and other quickie adult education classes, and I think the whole country should do the same.

But even without mandatory school courses in law, In Pro Per litigants can now learn the fundamentals of how to do battle in courtroom. This can be done by reading legal books written especially for laymen, such as the series published by Nolo Press and the like. These days, such courses are available on the Internet, VHS, and DVD, as well.

The Democratization of the Legal Process

The truth is, the courtroom really isn't that complicated. There is generally no math involved (except compounding the usury on alleged debts), and there are no equations to learn. The only laws one really needs to know are the Laws of the Law described in this book (which are also listed in Appendix B).

Once one has found one's bearing in the sea of statutes and codes and cases, it is fairly easy to navigate your way through the court process. You can get all the law in the universe at your fingertips for as little as $20 or a few hundred dollars per month by subscribing to a legal research online service, such as Jurisearch.com, Versuslaw.com, Westlaw.com, or LexisNexis.com. These days, legal research is far easier than in the old days, because the search engines in these online research services generally allow you to type in "natural language" to get the answer to all your questions, instantly.

If, for example, you want to know how much in late fees a bank can legally charge, all you have to do is type in "How much money in late fees can a bank charge legally on a credit card?"

Within seconds, the computer will magically bring up hundreds of cases, codes, statutes and the like, and all you have to do is "cite" them in your court briefs, to get what's coming to you.

Because of Newton's First Law of the Law, "for every opinion there is an equal and opposite opinion," you can always find a printed, precedent-setting case to suit your needs. All you have to do, then, is to argue that your own case is similar to that one. Then it is a crap shoot as to who wins . . . and creditors know this: No matter how much they have paid to highbrow legal mills to represent them, the outcome of any case is always unpredictable.

Add appeals and costs to the creditor, and you have an instant formula for winning your case In Pro Per.

Eventually, if you establish a winning track record, you may be able to convince a lawyer out there to take over the case on contingency, and even to pay your fees. Lawyers are always "hungry" for anything that promises to produce fees.

In the old days, one had to spend eons of time wading through stacks of heavy books in dusty law libraries to do legal research. Today, it's as easy as bidding on a Disney collectible on eBay.

The law has indeed become "democratized" through the Internet and modern technology. Today, there is no excuse for any debtor-litigant to fear the courtroom. All the weapons of war are at your fingertips.

Appendix A

List of Causes of Action a Debtor Can Sue a Creditor For

1. Fraud
2. Breach of contract
3. Violation of federal consumer credit protection act
4. Discrimination based on race, color, creed, age (over forty), gender
5. Reverse discrimination
6. Violation of federal and state fair debt collection acts
7. Antitrust violations
8. Bait and switch tactics
9. Infliction of emotional distress
10. Libel (including credit libel to agencies)
11. Slander (including credit slander to agencies)
12. Negligence

APPENDIX B

LIST OF LAWS
OF THE LAW

1. **Bruce Lee's Law of the Law:** Use jujitsu to turn a heavier opponent against himself by using his own momentum against him.
2. **Clausewitz's Law of the Law:** Litigation is the continuation of business by other means.
3. **Clint Eastwood's Law of the Law:** Even if the defendant wins, he loses because a huge legal bill must be paid.
4. **Cook's Law:** Litigants are "cooks" seeking to add as much spice and condiment to the stew as possible to increase the costs to the opposition.
5. **Copernicus's First Law of the Law:** The world of litigation will revolve around he who strikes first and most aggressively.
6. **Copernicus's Second Law of the Law:** Litigation tactics are analogous to gravitational forces in the real world.
7. **Eggshell Law of the Law:** A wrongdoer takes a victim as he finds him: with an eggshell head or a head of lead.
8. **Einstein's Law of Legal Relativity:** What one perceives as "truth" is relative to one's frame of reference, in every sense.
9. **Enron's Law of the Law:** There is no reason to feel guilty about stiffing a bad creditor, because you can safely assume that most creditors are as unethical as Enron executives.

10. **Fasces Law:** In great numbers, there is great strength.

11. **Frankenstein's Law:** Settlement agreements can create a monster of future litigation.

12. **Heisenberg's Uncertainty Principle of the Law:** It is never certain whether a person who signed a legal document had actually read it and comprehended it before signing it.

13. **Janitor's Law of the Law:** As part of any settlement with a creditor, a debtor must insist that his bad credit reports be erased.

14. **Judge Grumpy's Law of the Law:** Courts are not about "justice": Courts are about having someone make a decision when two sides can't decide the dispute for themselves.

15. **Kaiser's Law:** Arbitrators are all puppets of the industry that controls the arbitration process.

16. **King David's Law of the Law:** Most people will identify with the underdog and will cheer him on or join him [as in a class action], because there are always more underdogs than overdogs.

17. **Kipling's Law of the Law:** Ink is thicker than blood: If a harshly condemnatory story about a creditor appears in the newspaper or television, the indelible image created by that "ink" can serve to negate the bonds created by a mere "blood" signature on a contract.

18. **Law of Conservation of Money:** Money can neither be created nor destroyed. It can just change hands.

19. **Law of Entropy of the Law:** All settlements are arbitrary and chaotic, and chaos naturally increases.

20. **Law of Expert Sale:** An expert is hired to support the case of the side that pays his fees.

21. **Law of Inevitable Defects:** Every machine necessarily has some defects; no machine can be perfect.

22. **Law of Legal Supply and Demand:** Each year the law schools churn out far more lawyers than can find "real"

legal jobs in law firms, corporations, government agencies, and the like.

23. **Merry's Law of the Law:** The more defendants you sue, the merrier it is for you, because there will be a bigger pot of gold at the end of the rainbow (when it comes time to settle).

24. **Moses' Law of the Law:** In the Law, nothing is written in stone, except God's Ten Commandments.

25. **Multiplier Effect Law:** One individual debtor's damages may be relatively small, but become gargantuan when multiplied by millions of other debtors similarly situated in a class action.

26. **Napoleon's Law:** History is written by the winners.

27. **Newton's First Law of the Law:** For every trial verdict, there is an equal and opposite verdict based on the same facts.

28. **Newton's Second Law of the Law:** For each court opinion, there is an equal and opposite opinion somewhere in the law books.

29. **Newton's Third Law of the Law:** Whatever goes up in court, must come down.

30. **Pied Piper Law of the Law:** He who pays the piper expert witness calls the tune.

31. **Principal-Agent Law:** A principal is responsible for all acts of his agent.

32. **Puppet Law of the Law:** Legislators who enact laws are puppets of the industries that finance their campaigns.

33. **Reno-Hollywood Law of Jury Trials:** Verdicts are arbitrary and based on: (1) luck or chance; and (2) the histrionic talents of the witnesses.

34. **Roman Law of the Moving Target:** The less equity one has in his property, the less vulnerable the property is to seizure and plunder, and the safer one is from being sued.

35. **Simon Legree's Law:** If the landlord is sued by the tenant

for unsatisfactory property conditions, it is a mistake to seek to evict the tenant, because such efforts will generate only another lawsuit for retaliatory eviction.

36. **Sun Tzu's First Law:** In war, strategy and deception are of the utmost value . . . what counts is not what is seen, but what appears to be seen.

37. **Sun Tzu's Second Law:** Most battles are won before they have even begun.

38. **Truncator's Law of the Law:** Creditors will often arbitrarily reduce a debtor's credit limit, despite a sterling record of regular and consistent payments; this constitutes breach of contract and fraud by the creditor and should be met by cessation of all payments and a lawsuit by the debtor.

39. **Vince Lombardi's Law of the Law:** Winning isn't everything; it's the only thing.

40. **Wine Aging Law of the Law:** A lawsuit, just like a fine wine, gets better as it ages.

INDEX

medical collections—*continued*
  malpractice suits against, 76–82
  skyrocketing medical costs
    and, 72–74
money, fungibility of, 42, 45, 49
moneylending, ethics of, 4–6
mortgage lenders
  lawsuits against, 99–103
  public relations and, 103–7
  types of, 98–99
motion for summary judgment
  (MSJ), 177–82

N
national debt, 6

O
offshore asset havens, 69–70

P
perjury, 186, 188–89
political correctness, 122–23
Ponzi schemes, 28, 30
property transfers, 68–70, 108
prosecutors
  creditors and, 185–86
  suing, 187–88
protective orders, 111

R
relativity, law and, 57–59
repossession, of automobiles,
  109–14
retaliatory eviction, 117–19
reverse discrimination, 125–26

S
selective debt payment, 3
self-representation, 205, 207–9
settlements
  clauses in, 197–203

for clean credit history,
  198–203
confidentiality of, 199–202
court system and, 171–75
creditors' reasons for, 17–18,
  59–63, 166
future litigation and, 202–3
liquidated damages in, 200–1
negotiating, 161–66
Shakespeare's ghost scam, 24–26
Social Security number,
  obtaining new, 22–24
statute of limitations, 81
stockbrokers, suing, 133–39
stock market decline, 134–36
student loans, 2, 35, 87–90
suicide, 2
summary judgment motions,
  177–82
surcharges, 4

T
taxes
  avoiding, 69, 70
  owed to IRS, 2, 35, 91–96
  reduction of, for creditors,
    64–66
tax law, 93–94
tenant rights, 115–20
trusts, 67

U
U.S. tax court, 92
uncollectible debt, 64–66
United States, as debtor nation,
  6–7

V
vehicle defect litigation, 111–14
victimization, 151–55